UNLEASH
YOUR
MAGIC

Proven Strategies to Help Liberate
the Amazing Power Within

Dear Veena,
May you Unleash Your Inner Magic
to achieve your true meaning and
purposes in life.

With much love,

11 JULY 2022
MANCHESTER

LOGAN NAIDU

Foreword by
MARVIN FELDMAN

First edition 2014
Second edition 2015
Third edition 2022

Copyright © 2022 Logan Naidu

Published by Logan Naidu
www.logannaidu.com

Unleash Your Magic: Proven Strategies to Help Liberate the
Amazing Power Within / Logan Naidu
ISBN: 978-0-620-97634-3 (paperback)
ISBN: 978-0-620-97635-0 (e-book)

Cover design and typesetting by Gregg Davies Media
(www.greggdavies.com)

The 3rd edition of Unleash Your Magic is available as an e-book on all leading
digital platforms. Additional copies can be purchased from all leading book
retailers worldwide.

In Praise of *Unleash Your Magic*

Unleash Your Magic is a great masterpiece which talks about being blessed with incredible abilities and big dreams. It demonstrates how we can convert these dreams into reality by working on self-management, the right skills, and setting specific targets. Reading this book will help you create a clear vision of your goal, with more courage to make decisions upon encountering challenges so that you live out a wonderful life.

> — **Peggy Tsai,** RFP, CCFP, was MDRT MCC Region E Chair (China, Hong Kong/Macau, Taiwan) - 2022 First Vice President of MDRT's Executive Committee

Reading this book is indeed a 'magical experience' and I am already practicing some of the ideas in it. The writing style and passion for life is incredible to observe. I highly recommend this book to anyone who wants to understand MDRT better and be a part of this incredible organisation. The profound lessons contained in the book will also benefit all those who want to experience massive personal growth and development within any career or business. *Unleash Your Magic* will go down as one of the top five books I have ever read. Do not miss the opportunity to read and digest this amazing book by a gifted author.

> — **Kobus Kleyn,** Certified Financial Planner® professional, MDRT Top of the Table Member and Past MDRT Country Chair, South Africa

Unleash Your Magic is a source of new energy, truly inspirational. It is a condensed summary of wisdom and writings from leading personalities on this planet. This book is a must for all libraries and progressive individuals. Truly an elixir to propel your personal development! This summary of wisdom is true wealth, an intellectual energising experience.

> — **Dr Dylan K. Naidoo,** BSc Honours (Cum Laude), MB ChB (Natal), FC Derm (SA). Was one of South Africa's leading dermatologists and humanitarians

Unleash Your Magic is probably the most definitive description of the successful entrepreneur that I've ever read...No one can read the book without being optimistic about the future because it defines the unique role of being a success in your chosen field.

— **Manmohan Abdullah,** ChFC, CLU, RFP (Shariah), CIAM, MALAYSIA

Logan Naidu is a stalwart of our profession. He shows how tenacity and humility can bring lasting success to all of us prepared to see financial services as a calling and a life's career.

— **Tony Gordon,** United Kingdom, Past President, MDRT

I can understand that if you continue to step out of your own comfort zone, and stay at your best condition, you will be invincible. This is by far, one of my favorite books, which is full of inspiration and passion and I highly recommend reading it.

— **Joseph Fang,** MDRT MCC Zone Chair Taiwan

Logan is a man of knowledge and is very effective in imparting it to others.

— **Mehdi Fakharzadeh,** author and top sales professional

A must read for anyone in the financial industry. This book has really helped me to refocus and improve my foundation as a financial advisor. It is a truly inspiring book that focuses on what is important to help and advise people along their life journey and how to add value to their lives. It has helped me to be proud and inspired as a financial adviser, presenting great and practical examples of what one's mindset should be and value proposition should look like towards clients.

- **Jacques Mooij,** Financial Advisor, South Africa

Thanks to Logan's erudition, reading just one book 'Unleash Your Magic' is like walking into a library with little time and still benefitting a lot. A must-read book for people in the sales professions and those who seek the formula to a genuine balanced life of success.

- **Chris Feng**, Taiwan

I invited Logan to do a presentation to my team of agents. He spoke about visualization with such passion and conviction that I, and my team, made our own "visual commitment" to ourselves and my team doubled their production the very next month. And guess what, the Franchise production was exactly the amount I had visualized. We all loved the presentation and he certainly got my team thinking. I have read Logan's book, *Unleash Your Magic*, and given each of my team a copy as I believe it is a source of direction in all spheres of one's life.

— **Janine Petterson**, Business Executive, Discovery Financial Consultants, South Africa

I really like that Logan demonstrates how we can rise above self-imposed limitations and imagine our way to success and how we will be judged by the legacy we leave for future generations. Truly inspiring! Thanks for the awesome book!

— **Jose Antonio Soto**, California, USA

CONTENTS

FOREWORD

I have had the pleasure of knowing Logan for quite some time, and he is truly a steadfast supporter and believer in the Million Dollar Round Table.

Trying to convey the essence and spirit of MDRT Annual Meetings is virtually impossible, but Logan does a wonderful job of capturing many of the key ideas that have been presented at meetings he has attended during the course of his career. Among the many aspects covered in these pages, he provides an in-depth discussion of MDRT's 'Whole Person Concept', which encapsulates MDRT's philosophy of living a life of balance.

The chapters on visualization provide readers with a technique that enables them to set high goals and make those goals a reality. Logan outlines a step-by-step process to achieve this, supported by practical real-life examples. Applying and practising this technique will take your life to another level.

As we sometimes take life too seriously, this book will help you add more laughter and humour to your daily living and, in the process, add more years to your life. Some of the most powerful quotes by leading luminaries have been provided for inspiration and reflection.

The section on self-management highlights a powerful truth and clearly illustrates that this is the basis for managing and creating a successful life. Logan also shares a blueprint for success.

We are often judged by external indicators of success - our bank balance, the car we drive, the house we live in, the clothes we wear - but, in the end, we will be judged by the legacy we leave for future generations, and what we did to make this world a better place. It is the impact, the contribution and the positive difference we make in the lives of others that counts in the final analysis.

In the pages that follow, Logan implores readers to live their lives with purpose, and, through this book, you will have access to the material he shares to motivate and inspire international audiences.

MARVIN FELDMAN, CLU, ChFC, RFC
PAST PRESIDENT, MDRT

INTRODUCTION

"Man is made or unmade by himself; in the armoury of thought he forges the weapons by which he destroys himself; he also fashions the tools with which he builds for himself heavenly mansions of joy and strength and peace. By the right choice and true application of thought, man ascends to the Divine Perfection; by the abuse and wrong application of thought, he descends below the level of the beast. Between these two extremes are all the grades of character, and man is their maker and master."

— **James Allen – As A Man Thinketh**

The Million Dollar Round Table (MDRT), The Premier Association of Financial Professionals®, is a fascinating organization. There are many reasons MDRT inspires members, some of which are detailed below.

At the outset, it is important to remember that we're not policy peddlers. We're not product traders. We are service providers - we are love providers. We've learnt that the *only* way to be great is to serve others and we serve people because we love people. We care. Yes, the letters that are in our files and the gratitude that is in the hearts of those we serve attest to that love and humanness. Leo Buscaghlia, the eminent educator, author and lecturer, who graced the MDRT main platform in 1981 and 1986, spoke about it when he said:

"You know, I have a strong feeling that this wonderful quality of humanness, with all its wonders, is God's gift to you. And what you do with it is your gift to God. Don't satisfy yourself with anything less than offering God THE PERFECT GIFT THAT YOU ARE."

— Leo Buscaghlia

Becoming a member of MDRT and attending Annual Meetings can be a life-transformative experience. One gains friends across the globe and insights into every aspect of our profession. Since its formation, MDRT has positively impacted the lives of millions of individuals – members, their families and others.

Founded in 1927, MDRT is a global, independent association of the world's leading life insurance and financial services professionals from more than 500 companies in 70 nations and territories. MDRT members demonstrate exceptional professional knowledge, strict ethical conduct and outstanding client service. MDRT membership is recognized internationally as the standard of excellence in the life insurance and financial services business. For more information, visit mdrt.org and follow MDRT on Twitter @MDRtweet.

As a positive influence in the life insurance industry, MDRT has developed a rich tradition of sharing knowledge for the benefit of clients, prospects, advisors and companies.

Professional success is just one of the pillars of MDRT's levels of excellence. While members must meet a certain level of premium, commission or income during the year, they must also adhere to strict ethical standards.

A key differentiating factor is its philanthropic wing, the MDRT Foundation, the charitable arm of the Million Dollar Round Table. Exclusive to MDRT members, the MDRT Foundation has over a 60-year history of empowering members to be philanthropic leaders in their own communities and internationally, and has successfully contributed more than USD 38 million to organizations in 70 countries and all 50 US states, serving a diverse range of charitable causes around the globe. See www.mdrtfoundation.org.

To top it all, the MDRT Annual Meeting, the highlight of the MDRT calendar, is a unique, unrivalled event. It is MDRT's pinnacle conference, gathering thousands of members from around the world, in a spirit of camaraderie, to create an exclusive event like no other. Attendees hear inspiring speakers, learn insights from some of the best minds in the world and share their best practices and innovations with peers to help them attain new levels of success. The MDRT Annual Meeting is where members learn to be well-rounded individuals, improving their lives both personally and professionally. Lessons and stories from MDRT Annual Meetings are shared throughout this book.

> "I learnt this, at least, by my experiment: that if one advances confidently in the direction of his dreams, and endeavours to live the life which he has imagined, he will meet with a success unexpected in common hours."
>
> — **Henry David Thoreau**

MDRT's Whole Person Concept has impacted the lives of hundreds of thousands of members and their families. For some people, achieving a good work-life balance seems to come naturally. Yet, many constantly struggle to manage priorities in their professional and personal lives. As a successful financial services professional, are you leading the fulfilling and enriching life that you want? Or, do you recognize there are areas you may be neglecting or could improve? Refer to the valuable exercise in chapter 6.

Members attending Annual Meetings are encouraged to make a point of spending quality time with their families and helping their communities, countries and the world.

Having been exposed to profound presentations from the world's finest speakers at these meetings over many decades, this book is an attempt to share with readers some of the many lessons learned.

Every person in the financial services sector can rise above self-imposed limitations and inhibitions and *unleash the magic* that lies dormant within.

However, this book is not for members of the financial services industry only; the content and principles can help any person step out of the ordinary and power up to a higher level of excellence and success in their own life and career.

> "To be like the rock that the waves keep crashing over. It stands unmoved and the raging of the sea falls still around it."
>
> — **Marcus Aurelius**

This third edition of *Unleash Your Magic* has been totally revamped with further examples on **"Validation for Visualization"** (Chapter 4), a new chapter **'Reflections on Life and Living"** (Chapter 17) and a substantially revised chapter **"Unique Purpose in Life"** (Chapter 16). It was important to incorporate some of the profound lessons learned from the past six years of my **intensive studies on philosophy-spirituality** at the Vedanta Academy in Pune, India.

> "In oneself lies the whole world and if you know how to look and learn, the door is there and the key is in your hand. Nobody on earth can give you either the key or the door to open, except yourself."
>
> — **Jiddu Krishnamurti**

"Don't you know yet?
It's your Light that
lights the world."

— Rumi

In conclusion, a message to all readers whose parents are alive: do not wait until it's too late. Spend time with them - you will be amazed at the amount of wisdom they possess. Do not waste this precious opportunity. Have no regrets whatsoever when your parents or other loved ones pass on, which they will eventually do.

The one thing that all of us need to be aware of is that none of us has a lease on life. Every time we greet someone or say goodbye to somebody could be our last. Every breath we inhale could be our last, irrespective of age. So we need to make every encounter meaningful and ensure that every aspect of life counts. This is beautifully captured in this quote by ancient Greek philosopher Aristotle and in the quotes that follow.

"Thou wilt find rest from vain fancies if thou doest every act in life as though it were thy last."

— Aristotle

"Remembering that I'll be dead soon is the most important tool I've ever encountered to help me make the big choices in life. Because almost everything - all external expectations, all pride, all fear of embarrassment or failure - these things just fall away in the face of death, leaving only what is truly important."

— Steve Jobs

"Each morning we are born again.
What we do today is what matters most."

— Walt Disney

"Carpe diem! Rejoice while you are alive; enjoy the day; live life to the fullest; make the most of what you have. It is later than you think."

— Horace (Ancient Roman Poet. 65 BC to 8 BC)

In the pages that follow, it will be demonstrated that one can achieve whatever one wants out of life, irrespective of one's background, family circumstances or any other extraneous factor, as long as one gains knowledge, believes one can do it and then takes the necessary action.

One of the key techniques to achieve this is through the power of visualization (refer chapters 3 & 4). Each one of us has the creative genius within to be extraordinary. In fact, we have been designed and engineered to achieve greatness. In the pages that follow, some real-life experiences are shared with you.

"You see things and you ask, 'Why?' But I dream things that never were and I ask, 'Why not?'"

— George Bernard Shaw

FIRST EXPOSURE TO MDRT

"As a single footstep will not make a path on the earth, so a single thought will not make a pathway in the mind. To make a deep physical path, we walk again and again. To make a deep mental path, we must think over and over the kind of thoughts we wish to dominate our lives."

— **Henry David Thoreau**

Right at the outset of one's career in this great industry, one must realize that selling a policy is only the first step in a client-building relationship. The follow-up service is all important. Clients must know that, when they need help, you will be there. They must be able to count on you. Provide your clients with a level of service excellence that will delight them. Promise a lot - deliver more.

This is a noble profession. Helping clients with their financial planning is indeed more than a profession; it is a vocation. The benefits of our products enable people to live their lives in dignity. Life insurance, in particular, is more than just the purchase of an intangible - it truly is a gift of love. One will witness first-hand the wonderful benefits of this vocation. Financial professionals and advisors are endowed with the unique opportunity to make a positive, meaningful and lasting difference in peoples' lives. **Use It. "See the people! See the people! See the people,"** as the late great Ben Feldman advocated.

Be as professional as possible and act according to the highest ethical and moral standards. Study and acquire greater knowledge in all aspects of financial planning, ethics, and life in general. Remember: *'when you're green, you grow; when you're ripe, you rot'*.

By 1987, I had qualified for MDRT membership for six consecutive years and became a qualifying and life member (at that stage, this was the requirement for non-American members). I heard great things about the MDRT Annual Meeting and was determined to attend my first one.

A turning point in my career came about in 1987, when I attended my very first MDRT Annual Meeting in Chicago, USA. As it was relatively expensive to travel overseas, my wife Sussie and I decided to include a holiday as well. We booked coach tours on the US East Coast and West Coast for five weeks, which in itself was an amazing experience, this being our first visit to the US. Sussie then headed home and I continued on to Chicago.

"*MAGIC!*" This is how I opened my presentation to 200 delegates at the feedback presentation at Durban's Elangeni Hotel, a few weeks after returning home from the MDRT Annual Meeting. If there is one word that captures the atmosphere prevailing at an MDRT Annual Meeting, it is *'magic'* (refer to chapter 5 for more details). It is difficult to capture in words the profound impact this meeting had on my life. The magic of MDRT has stayed with me ever since. It was amazing to listen to and watch the world's leading advisers sharing their 'secrets' unselfishly. There were also many amazing non-industry speakers talking on every aspect of life including MDRT's Whole Person Concept and emphasis on 'Balance in Life'. One of the many things that attracted me to MDRT was the philosophy that our lives are not just about production or making money, but that there are many more aspects - physical, emotional, intellectual and spiritual - that need taking care of as well, to enable us to live full and meaningful lives.

> "The home should be the centre and not the boundary of affection. People make home a boundary of affection, so that affection and love may not go beyond that. The home should be the centre of affection so that rays of love may radiate in all directions"
>
> — **Swami Rama Tirtha**

Attending an MDRT Annual Meeting is undoubtedly an experience of a lifetime. One needs to be there in person to experience the glory of the event. The friendliness, humility and camaraderie evident all around is contagious. The entire atmosphere is electrifying, motivating, inspiring, unforgettable and dynamic. All delegates wear special name tags with their first names highlighted in large letters. One does not hesitate, for one moment, to shake hands and exchange ideas with fellow delegates, no matter where they come from. Everyone shares unselfishly. MDRT even has official greeters to make delegates feel special.

MDRT go out of their way to make first-time attendees (FTAs) feel at home. There is a special orientation for thousands of FTAs to familiarize them with the various activities and procedures, and to help them get the most out of the Annual Meeting. I was privileged to be a table host at a number of First Time Orientation sessions. The enthusiasm of the FTAs and all the other delegates one contacts is amazing to behold.

.... *Imagine* an event that would increase wealth, health and happiness.

.... *Imagine* friendship, warmth and camaraderie.

.... *Imagine* education, motivation and inspiration.

.... *Imagine* dreams come true.

This is what attending an MDRT Annual Meeting is about! I urge each and every reader who has not done so, to not only qualify for MDRT, but, more importantly, to attend an Annual Meeting. It is guaranteed to positively and significantly impact your life, and the lives of all those you touch, as it did mine and my family's. Share the powerful messages, lessons and ideas learned with your family and community and help to make a meaningful difference in their lives.

> "Let me not pray to be sheltered from dangers,
> but to be fearless in facing them.
> Let me not beg for the stilling of my pain, but
> for the heart to conquer it."
>
> — **Rabindranath Tagore**

Some incredible presentations were delivered from the main platform at MDRT Annual Meetings, one of which featured Rabbi Mark Gellman and Msgr. Thomas J. Hartmann at my very first meeting in Chicago. They were known as the GOD SQUAD and appeared on *Good Morning*

America and various other radio and TV programmes. They shared the following profound words of wisdom:

- Whatever is yours is others. Love and care for people other than selves. Be charitable with time more than money. Listen, help others and serve. You all do that admirably.

- Jarvish saying: *"Sticks in a bundle are unbreakable. Sticks alone can be broken by a child."* Take a bunch of pencils and try to break them - it is very difficult. Take one - it is easy to break.

- You can make a living by what you get; you make a life by what you give.

- *"It's not what you do, but what you are that makes you lovable."*

- Best speech (grandparent witnessing bar mitzvah): *"In your life, you're going to meet people who need your help. If you can help them, help them."*

- You can do well by doing good - help people, whether you're going to get something out of it or not.

- Say these words when experiencing 'problems' or difficult times: *"It's normal. It's natural. It will go away."*

- Greatest question, especially if someone is very angry: *"How long do you want to live like this?"*

- Anger is the most corrosive of all human emotions. *"Anger is like when **you** take poison and want someone else to die."* Angry people keep score of who did this, who did that that, who deprived them of their just desserts in life, etc. Ask them the greatest question.

- Know the price of sacrifice and be willing to pay it.

- Nobody becomes totally good/evil right away.

- There is something more in life. Also something more than life. This belief is shared by every religion.

- Mother Theresa: *"Don't do great things; do little things with great love."* She had a mission, motivated others, and did more with the resources she had.

> "We can easily manage, if we will only take, each day, the burden appointed for it. But the load will be too heavy for us if we carry yesterday's burden over again today, and then add the burden of the morrow to the weight before we are required to bear it."
>
> — **John Newton**

Let's talk about creativity. Do you think that you can teach creativity? The following story was shared by a speaker from the main platform at an MDRT Annual Meeting:

Let me recite a letter, recently received by the parents of a college student away from home for the first time. Many parents will be able to identify with this. The letter went like this: *"Dear Mom and Dad, sorry to be so long in writing lately, but all my stationery was burnt the night the demonstrators burnt the dormitory down. I'm out of hospital and the doctor says my eyesight should be back to normal sooner or later. That wonderful boy, Bill, who saved me from the fire, kindly offered to share his little apartment with me until the dorm is rebuilt. He comes from a good family, so you shouldn't be too surprised to learn, we're gonna get married. In fact, you always wanted to have grandchildren, so you should be really happy to learn you're gonna be grandparents next month."*

The letter then went on: *"Please disregard the above practice in English composition. There was no fire, I haven't been to the hospital, I'm not pregnant and I don't even have a boyfriend. But I did get a 'D' in chemistry and an 'F' in French and I wanted to make sure you received this news in the proper perspective. Love. Mary.*

Now, that's creativity. It is so important that we all use creativity and fun in our business.

Much more details on the 'Whole Person Concept, visualization techniques, MDRT Annual Meeting, keeping one's life in perspective, overcoming adversity, incorporating laughter into our lives, profound poems and quotes, secret of success, one's unique purpose in life, reflections on and lessons from my intensive philosophy-spirituality studies, and much more are covered in the chapters ahead.

> "The best and safest thing is to keep a balance in your life, acknowledge the great powers around us and in us. If you can do that, and live that way, you are really a wise man."
>
> — Euripides

TWO

MDRT AND PUBLIC SPEAKING

"Whatever you do, you need courage. Whatever course you decide upon, there is always someone to tell you that you are wrong. There are always difficulties arising that tempt you to believe your critics are right. To map out a course of action and follow it to an end requires some of the same courage that a soldier needs. Peace has its victories, but it takes brave men and women to win them."

— **Ralph Waldo Emerson**

We often hear the saying *'the universe operates in mysterious ways'*. One example of such a significant and unexpected development occurred at the 1996 MDRT Annual Meeting in Anaheim, California. A fellow qualifier, Bharath Purohit from Mumbai, India, came up to me during one of the breaks and we chatted for five minutes. He then asked me to speak at the forthcoming Life Insurance Round Table of India (LIRT) convention, which was to be held in Bangalore, India in just over two months' time. He indicated that LIRT would accommodate my wife Sussie and I in the finest hotels and would take us on a tour of some key places of interest in India. As I had never met Bharath before then and as he had not attended any of my presentations, and had no idea I was a speaker, I was completely taken aback, although I was grateful for the invitation to visit and speak for the first time in India. I told Bharath to send me a fax and I would confirm after my return to South Africa.

When I returned home around a week later, there was a fax on my table from Bharath: *"Dear Mr Naidu, thanks very much for agreeing to speak at the LIRT convention in Bangalore September 1-3..."*. He confirmed this was LIRT's Ninth Annual Convention and all our travel and accommodation arrangements were finalized.

I confirmed the speaking engagement with Bharat and LIRT President at that time, Mr PAL Kochhar, and Sussie and I flew to Mumbai. On arrival, we were accorded the greatest respect with both of us being garlanded, prior to heading to Bangalore. Our reception in Bangalore was amazing and we were treated like celebrities. Thus started my fascination with India.

I did two presentations at the LIRT convention that were really well received, sharing ideas and concepts I learnt from MDRT. MDRT membership in India at that stage was around 100. I spoke at length about the incredible benefits of MDRT membership, attendance at MDRT Annual Meetings, 20-point productivity plan, visualization techniques, etc. I also sent a motivational letter to all delegates after my return to South Africa, highlighting key points covered at the conference and encouraging them to put in the effort to qualify for MDRT membership. The impact of the presentations and subsequent letter was far greater than expected. It was astonishing that, with just over three months left to the end of the 1996 calendar year, dozens of attendees qualified for 1997 MDRT membership (based on 1996 production), a few becoming MDRT icons in India - see stories from just two agents who attended (Chapter 20) – R.K. Shetty and Laazarus Dias. I was invited back to present at LIRT's tenth annual convention at the Taj Mahal Hotel in Mumbai the following year (1997) and I subsequently spoke at a number of other LIRT meetings.

One of my fellow speakers in India was the late Peter Pond-Jones, who spoke at the 1995 MDRT Annual Meeting main platform on 'Triumphs and Tragedies', which included his battle with advanced cancer. We got on fabulously from the moment we first met and while we toured various parts of India.

Peter invited me to be a main platform speaker at the meeting of MDRT's European Chapter, which was held at The Barbican in London. It was a great honour to share the stage with the world-renowned Roger Bannister, who spoke on how he created history by being the first man in the world to break the four-minute barrier for the one-mile race.

*Logan meeting with fellow speaker Sir Roger Bannister at the
MDRT European Chapter Meeting in 1997*

Sussie and our three daughters, Sarisha, Linestha and Nevita, travelled with me. Peter and his wife, Brenda, insisted we stay at their lovely home in London, which we did.

When I was a regional general manager for Southern Life, I invited Peter and Brenda to visit South Africa, and he gave an incredible presentation as a keynote speaker at the annual convention I organised at my Company, Southern Life. On a later visit to London, I visited Peter in hospital, and, in spite of his indomitable spirit, valiant fight against his cancer and great sense of humour, he eventually succumbed to the disease.

Subsequently, I spoke extensively in India, including a two-hour presentation at a specially convened meeting of the Life Insurance Corporation of India (LIC) for their 200 top agents in Mumbai and numerous full-day seminars in Mumbai.

"Yesterday I was clever, so I wanted to change the world.
Today I am wise, so I am changing myself."

— **Rumi**

Due to growing awareness of MDRT and more MDRT speakers at seminars and conferences in India, MDRT membership increased exponentially to many thousands over the past two decades, reaching a peak in excess of seven thousand members during my term as MDRT Divisional Vice President.

I presented at MDRT Annual Meeting ConneXion Zones, an MDRT Experience Meeting in Kuala Lumpur, a Focus Session at the June, 2015 MDRT Annual Meeting in New Orleans and at various other parts of the world.

Much of the content of my presentations has been shaped by the valuable lessons I learnt from being part of MDRT. It has been such a privilege and honour to serve this great organisation, which makes a positive difference and impact in the lives of not only its members, but their families, friends and all others whose lives they touch. In this spirit, some powerful MDRT material is now within reach of a much wider audience through the publication of this book.

"He who would accomplish little need sacrifice little; he who would achieve much must sacrifice much. He who would attain highly must sacrifice greatly."

— **James Allen**

One of the most profound pieces of advice ever given is captured by William Shakespeare in his play, *Hamlet*:

POLONIUS' ADVICE TO LAERTES prior to his departure to France - *HAMLET*, ACT 1, SCENE 3

There, my blessing with thee.
And these few precepts in thy memory
Look thou character.
Give thy thoughts no tongue,
Nor any unproportion'd thought his act.
Be thou familiar, but by no means vulgar;
The friends thou hast, and their adoption tried,
Grapple them to thy soul with hoops of steel;
But do not dull thy palm with entertainment
Of each new-hatch'd, unfledg'd comrade. Beware
Of entrance to a quarrel, but, being in,
Bear 't that th' opposed may beware of thee.
Give every man thy ear, but few thy voice;
Take each man's censure, but reserve thy judgment.
Costly thy habit as thy purse can buy,
But not express'd in fancy - rich, not gaudy;
For the apparel oft proclaims the man,
And they in France of the best rank and station
Are of a most select and generous chief in that.
Neither a borrower, nor a lender be;
For loan oft loses both itself and friend,
And borrowing dulls the edge of husbandry.
This above all: to thine own self be true,
And it must follow, as the night the day,
Thou canst not then be false to any man.
Farewell. My blessing season this in thee.

WILLIAM SHAKESPEARE

This is a father's advice to his son on how to conduct himself in the world. It applies equally to all of humanity. Shakespeare cautions us not to verbalize all our thoughts, or put into action thoughts out of harmony or proportion with the occasion. Be friendly, but not common; do not befriend every chance newcomer. Avoid quarrels if you can, but, if they are forced on you, give a good account of yourself. Hear every man's opinion, but express your own ideas to few. Listen more than you speak. Dress well, but not ostentatiously. Neither borrow nor lend and guarantee yourself against being false to others by setting up the high moral principle of being true to yourself.

> "The man with insight enough to admit his limitations comes nearest to perfection."
>
> — **Johann Wolfgang von Goethe**

> "The best portion of a good man's life is his little, nameless, unremembered acts of kindness and of love."
>
> — **William Wordsworth**

THREE

VISUALIZATION

Of all the beautiful truths pertaining to the soul which have been restored and brought to light in this age, none is more gladdening or fruitful of divine promise and confidence than this—that man is the master of thought, the moulder of character, and the maker and shaper of condition, environment, and destiny.

— James Allen

One of my keynote presentations is titled 'Visualization'. I expand on the talk that was given by Louis Tice at my first MDRT Annual Meeting in Chicago, *'The Future Is There for Those Who Invent It'*, which impacted my life immeasurably. Visualization works – I have tried it many times and it works. What I'm about to share with you is so powerful that, if you take it to heart and believe it, without being sceptical, it can and will immensely impact your life!

"Imagination is everything. It is the preview of life's coming attractions."

— Albert Einstein

Louis Tice implored us to set goals and then to picture those goals in our mind. The vision in our mind must be vivid, experiential, as if we have already accomplished the goal. Initially, vision will not equal current reality - there will be a bit or a lot of disharmony or dissonance between the two. The thing about the mind is that a part of our subconscious always works to restore order. The creative genius within us resolves this gap between vision and current reality. Every one of us possesses this creative genius.

The normal procedure when we set goals is to follow up with the question: HOW? How am I going to achieve my goal? After listing all the resources required, one might feel overwhelmed and compromise on the goal, lowering it. He recommended something that radically differed with conventional wisdom. We must stifle the HOW. Do not ask HOW a goal will be achieved. Just visualise your goal. The HOW will work itself out automatically. Stick with your goal - don't compromise - otherwise, the subconscious mind will *not* go after that goal.

How does the mind do this? Each of us has, at the back of our heads, a reticular activating system, which acts as a filter - much like a good executive secretary who filters out mail and other information before passing on important items to the CEO. The reticular activating system takes into our brain information of value that will help achieve goals, and filters out information of no value. Let me give you a powerful example. I'll dramatize for effect. A mother has recently had a baby. She lives on a very busy street - lots of traffic 24 hours a day, near a busy airport with planes flying overhead all the time and, to compound matters, she has two teenage children who play loud music until the late hours of the night. You get the picture - a house with very high decibels of noise. The mother sleeps like a log through the high traffic noise, planes flying overhead and loud music, but let the baby stir and make the slightest sound - the mother is up in a flash. How can this be explained? The decibel level of the outside noise is perhaps 20 times the decibel level of the child's cry! Yet the mother hears the cry. It's the *value*, not the *volume*, of the information that's important, and *that* makes all the difference.

Louis Tice implored us to get into quantum thinking. It is a whole new way of thinking. We must rise above our conditioning. We must transcend. *We Can Invent the Future!*

As I said, this was 1987, my first MDRT meeting and my first exposure to this level of thinking. I was hungry for ideas; I was hungry for knowledge. I wanted to get the most out of the meeting, so I lapped up all the knowledge and *believed* every word spoken by Louis Tice. After all, he was regarded as one of the top four motivational speakers in the world and was said to be a consultant to half of the Fortune 500 companies at that time - so, who was I to disbelieve him? What did I do after the meeting? *I took action!*

> "As a man thinketh in his heart, so shall he be."
> "You are today where your thoughts have brought you;
> You will be tomorrow where your thoughts take you."
>
> — James Allen

I got back to South Africa and immediately set a goal to qualify for my company, Southern Life's, TOP 25 agents (out of 1, 000) the following year - something I had not only never achieved before, but never imagined I'd even qualify for. You see, my mental model told me that TOP 25 was reserved for a select few who were giant producers and who, naturally, made it every single year - I was really *not* in that league. So at the end of the 1987 - 1988 production year, after the results were announced, I sent a card to each of the TOP 25 qualifiers, and it read (my goal/vision was to qualify the following year): *"Sincere congratulations on qualifying for the TOP 25. Enjoy the trip."* I closed with these words: *"I will be joining you for next year's TOP 25 trip."*

At that stage I did not have a clue where the resources were going to come from. I stifled the 'HOW' as Louis Tice suggested. I did just what I was advised to do. I visualised myself and Sussie on the plane travelling to the Far East - the TOP 25 trip was to Singapore and Hong Kong - destinations we'd never been to. The process of visualization must be experiential; that is, in the *present* tense - in my case, *not 'I want to, wish to, hope to, have to, believe I can... achieve TOP 25'*, but *'I **have qualified for the TOP 25'**. The thing about the mind is that you can totally 'confuse' it - if you implicitly believe the 'pictures' you create in your mind, as if they have already happened, your mind does not know the difference between this and reality. The 'in' thing at that time was video cameras and they were very expensive to buy in South Africa. I visualised myself going into a video shop in Hong Kong and purchasing a Sony 8 mm video recorder. This and other pictures were realistic and firmly embedded in my mind as if they'd already happened. Remember what I said about the subconscious? Mine now had two pictures: one of me in Hong Kong/Singapore and the other of current reality. The mind always works to restore order.

Of course, the rest is history. Not only did I make Southern Life's TOP 25 that year, but many years thereafter... and, incidentally, a few of us went into a video shop in Hong Kong and purchased Sony 8 mm video recorders. Visualization works - I've tried it many times and it works. I guarantee, if you adopt it, it will significantly impact your life in amazing ways.

We can achieve anything we want in life provided we believe we can do it and take the necessary action. The only limitations are self-imposed. We might all be ordinary human beings, but each one of us is capable of doing extraordinary things.

One of the key goals in my first year in management in 1994 was to drastically increase our MDRT membership. I conducted regular two-hour MDRT sessions with financial advisers and any staff who were keen to attend. I co-ordinated all of the MDRT membership processing from my office, including articles in our monthly newsletter, and monitored figures on a monthly basis, among other things. I also encouraged use of our MDRT video library that I built up at Southern Life. What were the results? We succeeded in increasing the number of MDRT members in our region from seven to thirty in one year. In the second year, we increased this figure to forty, making twenty percent of Southern Life's agents in the province of KwaZulu-Natal MDRT members. When one considers that the worldwide average is less than 2%, this was indeed a major accomplishment. In 1995, we took up the largest number of Southern Life MDRT members and their spouses to the MDRT Annual Meeting in Toronto, Canada. For many of the agents, that was the first and, for some, their last experience of the magic of MDRT. They reminisce about it fondly to this day.

Managers who reported to me were also empowered, with phenomenal results. We created a culture of fun and productivity, with much more family involvement, in line with MDRT's philosophy. We formed a social club and organised a few family fun days and visits to the theatre, and so on. This proved highly successful.

Now let's get back to the power of the mind and visualization!

Dr Charles Garfield, who had a Doctorate in Mathematics, was fascinated with peak performers after watching astronauts at NASA rehearsing repeatedly, in a simulated environment, movements in conditions of zero gravity. He enrolled for a second PhD in psychology, studying peak performers. After extensive research on peak performers, both in sport and business, he concluded as follows:

> "Virtually all the athletes and other peak performers are visualizers. They see it; they feel it; they experience it, before they actually do it."
>
> — **Dr Charles Garfield**

How do they do this? They do it in their minds!

This concept was further reinforced by Gil Eagles at an MDRT Annual Meeting. He shared the principles of success. I will paraphrase his words: We think in pictures. We always - 100% of the time - act out the pictures. We humans have the incredible capacity to CHANGE those pictures. The subconscious mind doesn't know the difference. We need to set some goals; 98% of all our actions are automatic - 2% of our actions are the result of active thinking. Look through that little 2% window, because that's our power, our imagination, and we must do it with enthusiasm - we must see it. In order for us to grow, to become all that we are capable of being - to reach our goals, reach our potential, whatever that is for each one of us - we need to be willing to be uncomfortable for a while; eventually, it will become comfortable.

Follow through. We all fail. We all fall down. It's not how many times you fall down, but how many times you get up that matters. Always take two steps forward and one step backwards. Don't mark time.

JUST DO IT!

William James (1842 - 1910), the father of modern psychology, made the following profound statement over 100 years ago. This reinforces the concept of visualization.

> "There is a law in psychology that if you form a picture in your mind of what you would like to be, and you keep and hold that picture there long enough, you will soon become exactly as you have been thinking."

> — William James

FOUR

VALIDATION FOR VISUALIZATION

Deep within man dwell those slumbering powers; powers that would astonish him, that he never dreamt of possessing; forces that would revolutionise his life if aroused and put into action.

— **Orison Swett Marden**

Visualization is also called imagery or mental rehearsal.

If we need further corroboration to adopt this technique of visualization, there is substantial evidence to validate this. I will touch on a few examples of the power of visualization.

Arnold Schwarzenegger was crowned the greatest bodybuilder in the world, winning the Mr Universe title for six consecutive years. As a young athlete, Schwarzenegger swore by the power of visualization to reach his bodybuilding goals. *"It's all in the mind,"* he said. At one time, he had nothing except the belief that his mind was the key to getting where he wanted to go.

"I had this fixed idea of growing a body like Reg Park's (who won the Mr Universe title three times and starred in five films, featured as Hercules in four). The model was there in my mind; I only had to grow enough to fill it," he explained. "The more I focused in on this image and worked and grew, the more I saw it was real and possible for me to be like him. What you do is create a vision of who you want to be — and then live that picture as if it were already true."

"When I was very young, I visualised myself being and having what it was I wanted. Mentally, I never had any doubts about it. The mind is really so incredible. Before I won my first Mr Universe, I walked around the tournament like I owned it. The title was already mine. I had won it so many times in my mind that there was no doubt I would win it. Then, when I moved on to the movies, I did the same thing. I visualised myself being a successful actor and earning big money. I could feel and taste success. I just knew it would all happen."

— **Arnold Schwarzenegger**

Imagery or visualization has been described as "an experience that mimics real experience, and involves using a combination of different sensory modalities in the absence of actual perception". (*Advances in Applied Sport Psychology*" (Cumming & Ramsey, 2009, p. 5)).

Imagery is a psychological technique which has demonstrated its effectiveness in sport through positively affecting psychological states, such as decreasing anxiety and enhancing self-confidence, self-efficacy and concentration (Garza & Feltz, 1998; Post & Wrisberg, 2012). It is also beneficial for use as a coping strategy, maintaining existing skills, and reviewing past performances (Thelwell & Maynard, 2002; White & Hardy, 1998).

"If you can imagine it, you can achieve it. If you can dream it, you can become it."

— **William Arthur Ward**

Sports teams: Manning Rangers and Orlando Pirates

I got a surprise call from a colleague in the insurance industry one day. He wanted to know if I worked with and could motivate sports teams - in this case, it was football (soccer). I thought for a few seconds and realised that the principles are exactly the same, and told him *yes*. He then arranged for the owner and the team manager of Manning Rangers - Chico Lazarus and Param Joseph, respectively - to see me on Tuesday, 20 March 2001. They explained their team's precarious position of lying rock bottom in the Premier League in South Africa - that was *the* top league in the country. With just seven matches to go, Manning Rangers was facing relegation to the lower league. The difference in income generated would be more than 10 times less if that came to pass. They had played 27 matches, lost 16, drawn six games, and won just five matches. In the 27 matches, they scored 36 goals, but 54 goals were scored against them, leaving a negative difference of 18 goals - see the log table below. Things could not have been worse.

P	W	D	L	F	A	GD	PTS
27	5	6	16	36	54	-18	21

So these two gentlemen asked me if I could motivate the team before their match the next day, 21 March at 8 p.m., at the Chatsworth Stadium in Durban. We arranged a one-hour session for the team at the Umhlanga Hotel, in Durban's North Coast region at 11 a.m on the day of the match. I arrived at the hotel and the team was already assembled. Their body language - lazing around in the chairs with a depressing attitude and no smiles - did not give me too much hope that

I would achieve anything. For sessions like this, I normally play some high-powered music to get them active and to help change the mood and create some fun and laughter in the process. However, the music equipment was not working, so I was clearly not able to start with music, as I'd planned. That was a big setback, especially considering their negative state, which was, I suppose, to be expected after winning a paltry five out of 27 games - less than one win for every five matches played.

> "Your vision will become clear only when you can look into your own heart. Who looks outside, dreams; who looks inside, awakes."
>
> — C.G. Jung

My only other option, if I was to make any headway at all, was to do an exercise with them to gauge responsiveness and hopefully induce some laughter. Basically, I asked them to pick any one of three symbols - square, triangle or circle - and I shared findings by one of the world's leading research institutions based in the USA. This has a very humorous spin to it and I've done it with audiences all over the world, resulting in bursts of laughter. I got the same response here – they laughed heartily.

Once they had laughed and were all loosened up, I went into the visualization exercise in detail and, by the end of it, I was astounded to see that they were fully energized and highly motivated. I got them to visualise - *see, feel and experience* - winning the match that evening. Their opponents, African Wanderers, were one position above them, so, if they won this match, it would be a six-point difference - Manning Rangers +3 points versus African Wanderers –3 points.

While they were in this frame of mind, I asked them to visualise the winning margin and give me the number of goals they could visualise themselves scoring. They were so highly pumped up, a few blurted out 10-0. No team in the history of the league had won 10-0, and they themselves had never won a match that year by more than two goals. So, without trying to dampen their unbounded enthusiasm, I asked others what they visualised - a few more said 2-0, and others 4-0. We arrived at a consensus of 4-0 - Manning Rangers 4; African Wanderers 0. The team had never achieved anywhere near such a result the entire year, having scored an average of 1.3 goals per match, with an average 2 goals per match scored against them, in 27 games. It was an ambitious score line, but entirely achievable. To reinforce the vision of them winning 4-0, I asked them to shout out the number four, in unison, when I called out 'Manning Rangers'. When I said 'African Wanderers', they had to shout 0. This exercise went on for a few minutes and it seemed that they could not wait to get onto the field that evening.

> "A man is literally what he thinks, his character being the complete sum of all his thoughts."
>
> — James Allen

I got to the Chatsworth Stadium early and, 15 minutes before the match, the coach gave me a few minutes to motivate the team. I repeated the chant - 'Manning Rangers' and they shouted 'four'; 'African Wanderers' and they screamed '0'. This went on for a few minutes and the match started at 8:00 pm. I was sitting in the private box with the team's owner, Chico Lazarus, next to me.

Half-time came and there was no score. I went to the change room one last time and tried my best to pump them up - I again went through the 'Manning Rangers, 4; African Wanderers, 0' chant, and once again they were all fired up. The match resumed and, 20 minutes from the end, the score was still 0-0. I could sense Chico Lazarus getting more and more despondent - if they lost that game, Manning Rangers would be out of the Premier League, so nothing short of victory and three points would keep their fading hopes alive.

As the game progressed and the possibility of them winning 4-0 seemed more and more remote, Manning Rangers scored a goal. Five minutes later, they scored a second goal. Five minutes before the end of the game, they scored a third goal. Chico Lazarus turned to me and said, *"Logan, if they score a fourth goal, they will think you are The Lord himself."* Lo and behold, with just a minute to go, Manning Rangers scored a fourth goal and the score stood at 4-0. One minute into injury time, an African Wanderers player scored an 'own' goal, taking the final margin to Manning Rangers, 5; African Wanderers, 0, to great joy and celebrations. One bright spark of a player came up to me, all excited, and told me that I'd said they would score four goals. I asked him how many had *they* scored, and he had to sheepishly admit four goals, as their last goal had been scored by the opposition.

That 5-0 victory did wonders for the team's morale. I did another five sessions with them before each of their remaining games, except the last one. The league logs at the beginning and end of the six games were as follows:

P	W	D	L	F	A	GD	PTS
27	5	6	16	36	54	-18	21
33	9	7	17	49	59	-10	34

If we look at the team's results for the last six matches, they won four, drew one, and lost only one, accumulating 13 valuable points in the process, with a +8 goal difference, having scored 13 goals with just five goals scored against them.

P	W	D	L	F	A	GD	PTS
27	5	6	16	36	54	-18	21
33	9	7	17	49	59	-10	34
6	4	1	1	13	5	8	13

The net result was that Manning Rangers remained in the Premier League and avoided being relegated to the lower league that year. This reinforced the belief that visualization works in any situation.

A short while thereafter, I got a call from Mr Irvin Khoza, owner of Orlando Pirates - one of the two most glamorous and popular teams in South Africa - asking if I could come up to Johannesburg to motivate his team. Pirates were actually the number one team in the league at that time, but the team motivation was down and they were not winning every match. I did a one-hour session on visualization with the team on 7 May 2001, at the Sandton Sun Hotel in Johannesburg. I noticed Irvin Khoza and team coach, Gordon Igesund (past South African national soccer team head coach) conferring. I was then asked to extend the session for another hour. They were supposed to train that afternoon, but sacrificed the training to spend more time at the session. I did a few further sessions with Orlando Pirates and they went on to become league champions that year.

Visualization is a technique that enables us to access resources within that normally lie dormant. I think the great Indian Sage, Patanjali, captured this brilliantly over 2, 000 years ago when he pronounced:

> "When you are inspired by some great purpose, some extraordinary project, all your thoughts break their bonds; your mind transcends limitations, your consciousness expands in every direction, and you find yourself in a new, great and wonderful world. Dormant forces, faculties and talents become alive, and you discover yourself to be a greater person by far than you ever dreamed yourself to be."

— Patanjali (c. 1st to 3rd Century B.C.)

What a powerful and inspiring declaration. This clearly directs us to have a higher purpose in life, to set high goals and visualise extraordinary achievements - when we do so, as Patanjali says, our mind and intellect are no longer constrained by limitations, there is an expansion of our consciousness and we then discover a *new, great and wonderful world*.

I am going to make a bold, perhaps provocative statement. In my experience, I would say that most people's reticular activating system is dormant, and thus *not* available to help us achieve a great purpose or extraordinary project. Why this assertion? Well, you will remember that the reticular activating system acts as a filter, letting in things of value and filtering out stuff that's of no value. It thus stands the test of rationality that there's got to be some kind of 'reference point' that would enable the reticular activating system to perform the function it has been designed for.

It is reasonable to submit that the 'reference point' is having a vision of what we want to achieve in our lives. Once the vision - experiential, present tense - is set, this then allows the reticular activating system to determine what information or resources to allow into one's consciousness, and what to filter out with a view to achieving our set vision. Reason and logic, therefore, suggest that, without a vision, the reticular activating system lies dormant... dead, for all intents and purposes. So, we have a part of our human composition that is unbelievably powerful, beyond our wildest imagination, yet most people do not make use of this inherent attribute.

The clear message to every reader is this: start using visualization techniques to achieve meaningful goals in every area of your lives. Set the bar high, as Michelangelo so eloquently expressed over 500 years ago:

> "The greater danger for most of us is not that our aim is too high and we miss it, but that it is too low and we reach it."
>
> — **Michelangelo**

Visualization is used by Michael Phelps, the most successful and most decorated Olympian of all time with a total of 28 medals. Phelps holds the all-time records for Olympic gold medals, Olympic gold medals in individual events, and Olympic medals in individual events. Visualization is also used by Katie Ledecky, who is considered one of the greatest female swimmers of all time, having won 7 Olympic gold medals and 15 world championship gold medals, the most in history for a female swimmer. Renowned talk show host, television producer, actress, author, and philanthropist Oprah Winfrey has used this technique, as well as business titan Sarah Blakely, among many others.

"One of the things that has been good for me I think, besides training, has been my sort of mental preparation," Phelps said of the technique.

Ledecky has said: "I have my goals and I visualize things to help me achieve those goals ... I know what my stroke should feel like at different parts of the race, and I can just kind of picture that in my mind."

Oprah Winfrey credits visualization with landing her celebrated role in *"The Color Purple."* Besides frequently showcasing success stories of positive thinking on The Oprah Winfrey Show — and even discussing creating her own vision boards to realize her dreams — her many words of wisdom to fans include: "Create the highest, grandest vision possible for your life, because you become what you believe" and "If you can see it and believe it, it is a lot easier to achieve it."

> "A man sooner or later discovers that he is the master-gardener of his soul, the director of his life."
>
> — **James Allen**

Will Smith is a big advocate of the law of attraction. The award-winning actor says his positive thinking has helped him achieve happiness. "In my mind, I've always been an A-list Hollywood superstar. Y'all just didn't know yet," Smith has said of the visualizing techniques that helped him along the way. He's also fond of quoting Confucius's motivating motto, as a way of explaining his blockbuster success: "He who says he can and he who says he can't are both usually right."

In the early 1990's, Jim Carrey was an unknown actor, broke and poor, struggling to get by. To stay motivated, he decided to write himself a check for $10 million for *"acting services rendered,"* dated it for Thanksgiving 1995, and carried it in his wallet for daily inspiration. In November 1995, shortly before Thanksgiving, Carrey found out he was cast in the movie *"Dumb and Dumber"* for — you guessed it — $10 million. Today, Carrey is one of America's top movie stars and he credits his constant visualization with helping him get there.

> "I would visualize things coming to me. It would just make me feel better. Visualization works if you work hard. That's the thing. You can't just visualize and go eat a sandwich."

> — **Jim Carrey**

Many athletes, from grassroots level up to elite sports personalities, have turned to the power of visualization or **imagery** to give themselves an edge over the competition. The difference between qualifying for a medal and falling short seems to come down to the **mental game**. For example, Brazilian footballer Ronaldinho employs imagery for game preparation and strategy purposes. Considered one of the best players of his generation and regarded by many as one of the greatest of all time, Ronaldinho won two FIFA World Player of the Year awards and a Ballon d'Or. A global icon of the sport, he was renowned for his technical skills, creativity, dribbling ability and accuracy from free-kicks:

> "When I train, one of the things I concentrate on is creating a mental picture of how best to deliver the ball to a teammate, preferably leaving him alone in front of the rival goalkeeper. So what I do, always before a game, always, every night and every day, is try and think up things, imagine plays, which no one else will have thought of, and to do so always bearing in mind the particular strength of each team-mate to whom I am passing the ball. When I construct those plays in my mind I take into account whether one team-mate likes to receive the ball at his feet, or ahead of him; if he is good with his head, and how he prefers to head the ball; if he is stronger on his right or his left foot. That is my job. That is what I do. I imagine the game".

Former England rugby international fly-half, Jonny Wilkinson, uses imagery as an important mental preparation technique. He talks about how he listened to a pre-recorded imagery script (another method of employing visualization) before the 2003 World Cup Final:

> "I surface for my usual pre-match ritual of a shave and shower before settling down to listen to a mental rehearsal CD. The script is prepared by myself and my coach but read by him. This visualization technique is a sort of clarified daydream with snippets of the atmosphere from past matches included to enhance the sense of reality. It lasts about twenty minutes and by the end of it I feel I know what is coming. The game will throw up many different scenarios but I am as prepared in my own head for them as I can be. If you have realistically imagined situations, you feel better prepared and less fearful of the unexpected".

India's top javelin thrower, Neeraj Chopra is the first track and field athlete to win a gold medal for India, which he did at the Tokyo Olympics held in 2021. Even before he got to Japan, Chopra said he has already had a few rounds of throws at the Olympic Stadium in Tokyo, where the men's javelin qualifying began on August 4. The 23-year old sits in a quiet space, imagines he's walking into the Tokyo Olympics Stadium. He gets ready, makes his approach run and lets the javelin soar. Chopra practiced the art of visualization and played this scenario in his mind for months leading up to the Tokyo Olympics. He had been there for a while, mentally at least.

> "I keep visualizing my throws in Tokyo. I imagine the setting and the area and how I will perform. I do this so that it won't feel like a new experience when I am actually there and so that I won't be overwhelmed by the situation," he said. "I felt as if my body was in flames," Chopra said later. "There was so much energy in me."

Chopra was the second person to throw in the final. He came charging in and it all clicked - the run smooth and fast, then the strong brake with his front leg, the whole energy from the run uncoiling behind it and into his throwing arm. A massive 87.03m. It immediately put the other eleven throwers under pressure. His second throw was even better at 87.58m, and Chopra knew it immediately, roaring in joy even before the javelin had landed. The Gold Medal was his.

The following is an extract from an article by Christopher Clarey in the NEW YORK TIMES reporting on the 2014 Russian Olympics in Sochi:

The Canadian bobsledder Lyndon Rush had not yet arrived in Sochi. But he was already on the Olympic sliding track as he sat in a chair in the Munich airport several days before the Winter Olympics, his eyes wide open but his mind's eye far away as he traced a sinuous path through the air with his left hand. *"I just went from 7 to 14,"* Rush said, referring to the section of the track between Curve 7 and Curve 14.

Visualization has long been a part of elite sports. Al Oerter, a four-time Olympic discus champion, and the tennis star Billie Jean King were among those using it in the 1960s. But the practice of mentally simulating competition has become increasingly sophisticated, essential and elaborate, spilling over into realms like imagining the content of news conferences or the view from the bus window on the way to the downhill. *"The more an athlete can image the entire package, the better it's going to be,"* said Nicole Detling, a sports psychologist with the United States Olympic team.

This is, more than ever, a multisensory endeavor. *"You have to smell it. You have to hear it. You have to feel it, everything,"* said Emily Cook, the veteran American aerialist and six-time US champion, who has competed in two prior Olympics and was ranked second in the world cup aerial skiing standings.

"Go confidently in the direction of your dreams.
Live the life you have imagined."

— Henry David Thoreau

TD Bank ranks among the world's leading online financial services firms, with more than 15 million active online and mobile customers. According to a TD Bank Survey, one in five small business owners used some form of a vision board (also referred to as an action board) when they started their business. Of these, seventy-six percent say that their business is now where they had envisioned at the beginning.

Vision boards work because our brain is malleable and trainable; it can even rewire itself. This remarkable capacity is referred to as neuroplasticity, and it allows us to train our brain for success. Visualization is one of the most powerful and efficient ways to do this. The rewiring process harnesses two key components: mirror neurons and neural resonance. Mirror neurons are vital to the learning process and planning our actions, as well as understanding the intentions behind them. Neural resonance is involved in focus and problem-solving. Visualization can help us to rewire our brains resulting in greater access to ideas, solutions, and motivation.

Not only is it important to visualize the success, but also the steps it takes to get there. We know that the brain sees little difference between a powerfully imagined vision and the actual experience of the vision coming to fruition. That's why athletes can significantly improve their performance as they "see" extreme workouts and their body growing stronger and more agile. They see, feel, and smell how it feels to win, and even to break world records.

The 2015 FIFA Women's Soccer World Cup Final between Japan and the United States was held on 5 July 2015 in Vancouver, British Columbia, Canada. The U.S. women's soccer team, looking for revenge after a devastating loss in 2011 at the hands of Japan, dominated the World Cup final. The Americans beat Japan 5-2 for their record third championship and first since 1999. While training just before the final, Carli Lloyd, who was named the World Cup's most outstanding player, said she mentally visualized herself scoring four goals. She went on to score a hat trick - the first woman in World Cup history to do so - as the U.S. burst to a four-goal lead in the first 16 minutes. "When you're feeling good mentally and physically, those plays are just instincts," Lloyd told The New York Times. "It just happens."

Kerri Walsh and Misty May-Treanor, the most successful female beach volleyball team in history — say they often rely on visualization to stay focused in the sand. They have three Olympic gold medals under their belts. "A lot of what we do is visualization," Walsh told USA Today. "To be able to take in the sights, the sounds, the stress, the excitement — that's going to serve us really well moving forward."

Lindsey Vonn, one of the most successful female gold medalist skiers in history, says her mental practice gives her a competitive advantage on the course. "I always visualize the run before I do it," Vonn said. "By the time I get to the start gate, I've run that race 100 times already in my head, picturing how I'll take the turns." "I love that exercise," Vonn has said. "Once I visualize a course, I never forget it. So I get on those lines and go through exactly the run that I want to have."

"If you can dream it, you can do it."

— Walt Disney

Dr. Jennifer Cumming, University of Birmingham, who studied how the best athletes use imagery, states that imagery is most beneficial when it is:

- Vivid and detailed

- Incorporates all senses (see, feel, hear, smell, and taste)

- Occurs in "real-time"

- Has positive focus

She provides the following tips for getting started:

- **Practice makes perfect**. Imagery is a skill, and, just like any skill that you perform in your sport, you will need to practice in order to be perfect.

- **Quality... not quantity**. Because imagery is a mental skill, you will need to concentrate on creating and controlling your images, which can be tiring when you first get started. For this reason, it is best to begin your imagery training by imaging high quality images for short periods of time, and then gradually increasing the time you spend imaging.

- **Set the scene**. Try to make your imagery as realistic as possible by re-creating important details of your sport setting (e.g. practice and competition venues) in your mind's eye. By including details like the colour of your opponent's uniform or the sound of the spectators' cheering, you will feel like you are really experiencing the performance that you are imaging.

- **Plan your imagery.** Images of your sport can frequently pop into your head, but to really benefit from imagery, you should plan the content of your imagery to meet your current needs.

- If you are struggling to perform a certain skill or strategy in game situations, you should try imaging yourself performing that skill or strategy perfectly and confidently in an upcoming game.

"The vision you glorify in your mind,
The ideal that you enthrone in your heart -
This you will build your life by,
This you will become."

— James Allen

FIVE

THE MDRT ANNUAL MEETING

"The two most important days in your life are the day you are born and the day you find out why."

— **Mark Twain**

As I mentioned at the outset, if there is one word that describes the atmosphere prevailing at an MDRT Annual Meeting, it is 'magic'. Those of you who have attended an MDRT Annual Meeting will agree. Through its meetings, MDRT provides attendees networking and idea sharing opportunities that lead to personal and professional advancement. The MDRT Annual Meeting, Top of the Table Annual Meeting, MDRT EDGE and the MDRT Global Conference have proven to be the foundation of MDRT — bringing together a community of premier financial services professionals and providing innovative content, first-class industry speakers and unparalleled networking experiences.

The warm smiles and friendly handshakes that greet delegates on their arrival at the registration desk immediately set the tone for the rest of the meeting. The glorious opening ceremony - usually featuring an array of singers and dancers - is phenomenal. The MDRT Annual Meeting gathers thousands of members from around the world to create an exclusive event like no other that stimulates growth through learning, networking and sharing innovative ideas. Attendees hear inspiring speakers, learn insights from some of the best minds in the world, and share their best practices and innovations with peers to help attain new levels of success. The MDRT Annual Meeting is where MDRT members learn to be well-rounded individuals, improving their lives both personally and professionally. Being a part of that magnificent gathering is an unforgettable and moving experience. In spite of the large number of delegates who attend, every delegate is made to feel important, special and equal. One is able to mingle with, meet and talk to successful, enthusiastic colleagues from every corner of the world. At my very first meeting in Chicago, in 1987, I was indeed privileged to shake hands with the great Ben Feldman, and have my picture taken with him. Ben Feldman was regarded as a living legend in America. He was rated one of the world's greatest and most successful financial services professionals of all time. Everywhere he went, hundreds of delegates would gather around him for autographs. I'm certain some of his success rubbed off on me; since returning from that meeting, not only did my production double, but it gave me a new perspective on life.

Logan meeting the legendary Ben Feldman at the 1987 MDRT Annual Meeting in Chicago

It was incredible to listen to the great Ben Feldman sharing, word for word from the main platform, how he interacts with clients. It was truly revealing and inspiring. Ben's generosity of spirit and unselfishness in openly revealing his 'secrets of success' epitomises the spirit of MDRT.

The main MDRT sessions are very extensive. Although the format has evolved in recent years, most of the meetings I attended commenced with breakfast sessions from 6 a.m., followed by main platform sessions commencing at 8 a.m. on most days. This ends at about noon, followed by a sales ideas lunch. The selection of main platform speakers is unbelievable. They are the very best in their field, the *crème de la crème* from different parts of the world. There are also concurrent afternoon Focus and Special Sessions. Although delegates are occupied virtually the whole day, they thoroughly enjoy every moment. The sessions are motivational, educational and inspirational. Earlier MDRT meetings had an entertainment showcase - featuring singing and musical talent from within MDRT membership. This spectacular event was held on the Wednesday evening and it was an honour to perform at five such showcases - singing some of my favourite songs.

> "He that has light within his own clear breast
> May sit in the centre, and enjoy bright day:
> But he that hides a dark soul and foul thoughts
> Benighted walks under the mid-day sun;
> Himself his own dungeon."

> — **John Milton**

Recent **MDRT Annual meetings** included Main Platforms, Cornerstone presentations, MDRT SPEAKS, ConneXion Zone, Idea Exchange, Echo Sessions and Special Sessions. Due to the Covid-19 pandemic, the 2020 MDRT Annual Meeting and Global Conference I attended was a Virtual Event held from August 3 – 7. The October 21 – 23, 2021 Top of the Table Annual Meeting was held 'live' at Amelia Island, Florida, with 200 members in attendance, while others attended virtually, as I did.

MDRT is working hard to find ways to get you the content you need to keep your business moving forward and overcome the challenges you and your clients are facing.

Going back to a much earlier time, Tom Wolff, a legend in the industry, quoted John Gardner, former US Secretary of State, when he said the following at the 1968 MDRT meeting: "The cynic says 'one man can't do anything'. I say 'only one man can do anything'." "All good ideas start with one man. The best piece of advice I ever received was given to me by one man, not by a crowd, not by a corporation, not by a parliamentary body, by just one man, not famous, not terribly important, but capable of saying something to me at a time when I needed it."

One man interacting creatively with others can move the world. The creative, caring, believing person sends out waves of influence.

Most of our corporations, if you trace their history back through the acquisitions and mergers, began with one man. Most of the significant innovations in the world can be traced back to one man with an idea.

Another profound piece of advice delegates hear at most meetings is that we should not wait until we are terminally ill to appreciate those around us - our friends, our parents, our children or clients.

> As a being of Power, Intelligence, and Love, and the lord of his own thoughts, man holds the key to every situation, and contains within himself that transforming and regenerative agency by which he may make himself what he wills.
>
> — James Allen

Then there is the concept of 'giving'. There is probably no business institution than MDRT that better exemplifies and tries to teach its members a philosophy behind the real meaning of giving.

Each of us has three main things available to us to give: our time, our talents and our treasure. In the book *The Prophet*, Kahlil Gibran says: "You give but little when you give of your possessions. It is when you give of yourself that you truly give."

"It is every man's obligation to put back into the world at least the equivalent of what he takes out of it."

— Albert Einstein

There are three main points about giving. The first is that each of us has an obligation to give, to make the world a better place than we found it. Second, we have an obligation to teach our children about giving, and the most powerful teacher teaches by example. Finally, there is the exciting paradox about giving. When you are giving for the right reasons, it is impossible to give anything away; it always comes back to you in wonderful, exciting ways that you cannot possibly predict.

"We must give more in order to get more. It is the generous giving of ourselves that produces the generous harvest."

— Orison Swett Marden

One of the most powerful treatise on 'giving' is by Lebanese poet and philosopher, Kahlil Gibran, in his multi-million best-seller book, The Prophet, which is quoted below in its entirety.

ON GIVING - BY KAHLIL GIBRAN

You give but little when you give of your possessions.
It is when you give of yourself that you truly give.
For what are your possessions but things you keep and guard for fear you might need them tomorrow?
And tomorrow, what shall tomorrow bring to the over-prudent dog burying bones in the trackless sand as he follows the pilgrims to the holy city?
And what is fear of need but need itself?

Is not dread of thirst when your well is full, thirst that is unquenchable?

There are those who give little of the much which they have - and they give it for recognition and their hidden desire makes their gifts unwholesome.
And there are those who have little and give it all.
These are the believers in life and the bounty of life, and their coffer is never empty.
There are those who give with joy, and that joy is their reward.
And there are those who give with pain, and that pain is their baptism.
And there are those who give and know not pain in giving, nor do they seek joy, nor give with mindfulness of virtue.
They give as, in yonder valley, the myrtle breathes its fragrance into space.
Through the hands of such as these, God speaks, and from behind their eyes He smiles upon the Earth.

It is well to give when asked, but it is better to give unasked, through understanding.
And to the open-handed, the search for one who shall receive is joy greater than giving.
And is there aught you would withhold?
All you have shall someday be given.
Therefore, give now, that the season of giving may be yours and not your inheritors'

You often say, "I would give, but only to the deserving."
The trees in your orchard say not so, nor the flocks in your pasture.
They give that they may live, for to withhold is to perish.
Surely he who is worthy to receive his days and his nights is worthy of all else from you.
And he who has deserved to drink from the ocean of life deserves to fill his cup from your little stream.
And what desert greater shall there be than that which lies in the courage and the confidence, nay, the charity, of receiving?

And who are you that men should rend their bosom and unveil their pride, that you may see their worth naked and their pride unabashed?

See first that you yourself deserve to be a giver, and an instrument of giving.

For in truth it is life that gives unto life - while you, who deem yourself a giver, are but a witness.

And you receivers - and you are all receivers - assume no weight of gratitude, lest you lay a yoke upon yourself and upon him who gives.

Rather rise together with the giver on his gifts as on wings.

For to be over mindful of your debt is to doubt his generosity who has the free-hearted earth for mother, and God for father.

KAHLIL GIBRAN

"The best way to find yourself is to lose yourself in the service of others."

— Mahatma Gandhi

You must know what you want, so that, when you get it, you know it. You must have goals. It's been said: *"If you don't know where you're going, you'll probably end up some place else."*

Make every minute count!

Do the things that failures don't like to do!

Fifty percent of your day, each day, should be spent face to face with clients – personally or virtually, helping with their financial planning. The other 50% should be spent on education, paperwork, follow-up and so on. **However, the single, most important action is to see the people.** MDRT stalwart, the late Sid Friedman's 10 little words are indeed profound: **"IF IT IS TO BE, IT IS UP TO ME."**

A central philosophy of MDRT is to inculcate in members the need for a balanced life, the need to be a whole person. We must carefully weigh the cost of success. Speaker Rabbi Harold Kushner made a profound observation at my very first MDRT Annual Meeting in 1987: "It's no use reaching the top if you have no one to share it with." It would undoubtedly be an empty feeling, a hollow victory.

Never ignore family or your health. Never get so busy making a living that you forget to make a life.

A question that we should constantly ask ourselves is this: If we were on trial for being financial advisers, would there be enough evidence to convict us? To put this another way, how much of each day is spent in the key activities required of a financial adviser?

Have any of you ever been bitten by an elephant? Of course not! It's the mosquitoes and bees that bite (little things), not the elephants. The same is true in your life and in the financial services business. It's the little things that go wrong that can cause you difficulty, and it's the little things done right that earn you the big results. Focus on little things you already know, never forgetting that it's not what you know that counts - it's what you **do** and **how** you do it. Action is the key. Look for little things you can improve to be more effective, to be a better financial services professional and to achieve more of your goals.

For example:

- Always operate according to the highest moral, ethical and professional standards of excellence.

- Improve your knowledge and have a positive mental attitude.

- Make a positive difference in the life of one more person daily.

- Become a member of a recognised professional financial planning association in your country and achieve a certified qualification in this industry.

- Attend at least one MDRT Annual Meeting.

- Do comprehensive needs analyses to establish clients' needs.

- Help clients resolve their financial planning shortfalls.

- Genuinely care for your clients and get to know them better so that you can serve them better.

- Set aside quiet time for yourself.

"I slept and dreamt that life was joy. I awoke and saw that life was service. I acted and behold, service was joy."

— **Rabindranath Tagore**

Remember that: "a person who is wrapped up in himself/herself makes a small package."

I identify with the following three sayings picked up at an MDRT Annual Meeting over 25 years ago:

"People don't care how much you know, until they know how much you care."

"It's nice to be important, but it's more important to be nice."

"Be nice to little people; you're still one of them."

It's important to use humour in our daily lives. Laugh at the things you cannot change and, please, don't take yourself too seriously. If you didn't do well at school, laugh off your poor academic performance by stating that you graduated in the half of the class (bottom half, of course) that made the top half possible.

Some other humour from MDRT speakers:

- Former USA Republican President, Ronald Reagan, to doctors after being shot: *"I hope you're all Republicans."*

- When appointments cancel, sales fall through, your luggage is lost, or someone says *'I'm from the tax office and I'm here to audit you'*, LAUGH. What else can you do? To really have a good laugh:

- Get out your old high school or wedding pictures.

- Remember that the size of your funeral will be determined by... you've got it - the weather.

LORETTA LA ROCHE, a main platform speaker, was dynamic and had an amazing sense of humour.

She spoke about 'awfulising' and 'catastrophising' minor events. Instead of people taking cell phones to the beach, they should take sand to the office. She said that the big challenge is bringing sanity back to an insane world. There is more depression now than ever before. People don't have fun. You're going to die anyway. Life's amazing and everyone is a joke. Don't go around saying *'I'm important'* or *'I'm a manager'* - who cares? Smile and laugh - it changes one's physiology.

Don't wait for anything. You never know. Get out of the box and move away. Don't be small - enlarge. When you die, people must say *'he was all used up'*. People don't see our joy. She suggested we scream

'WHIPPEE'! It drives our energy up. Try it! Loretta walks through the first class cabin in planes and loudly proclaims, *"Peasant coming through."*

She got all delegates to sing in unison, *"If you're happy and you know it, clap your hands."* Do this three times and watch your energy levels rise.

She then offered this sound reality:

If we think the worst and get the worst, we suffer twice.

If we think the best and get the worst, we suffer once.

CAREY HAUENSTEIN, former MDRT President, had this to say in his Presidential Address:

"We do not just distribute life insurance. We are more than just the sum of our sales. We form the raw material to fit a thousand emotional and financial shapes. We are sculptors who work with grand dreams and terrible fears to create invisible monuments. We are students locked in a lifelong study of a world where basic human nature collides with complex financial science. At its best, our work is a gift whose compensations lie beyond any commission scale. And though the rewards may be vast, the demands are awesome. You cannot work with the very souls of others without facing your own."

He went on to talk about what he thought the performance equation would be for the successful producers of the new era. These men and women will be superbly trained, highly educated, deeply compassionate and extremely efficient. Of course, so will their less successful counterparts.

However, the best performers will possess two qualities that will lift them above the rest. He believed those qualities to be *pride* and *principle.* There is no shortage of pride *within* this industry, but there is far too little pride *in* this industry. We are fiercely proud of what we achieve, yet sometimes too embarrassed to tell a stranger how we make a living. We complain that the public doesn't admire what we do, but show too little admiration ourselves for what we do. Let's start talking more about what we're doing well than how well we're doing. Let's surround ourselves with people who are prouder of their profession than their pay cheque. Work to bring out the best in yourself and your competition. Pull the competition up to your level.

We need strong principles every bit as much as healthy pride. Dwight Eisenhower said, "A people that values its privileges above its principles soon loses both. Principle goes by many names. Some say it's a matter of conscience; others, integrity, excellence, standards. And it stands alone in final judgment as to whether we have demanded enough of ourselves, and, by that example, have inspired the best in those around us."

20-Point Plan

Carey Hauenstein shared one of the most powerful activity generators I have come across - the 20-Point Plan. I have used it personally and I know many other advisers who have done so. It is highly effective.

If you implement this system that Carey introduced, it is virtually guaranteed that you will witness a significant increase in productivity.

This is how the points are accumulated.

1 point for each referral/telephone call you make for an appointment.

2 points for securing an appointment.

3 points for every face-to-face (or virtual) client meeting.

4 points for every attempt at closing (see criteria below).

5 points for every sale.

The points can be accumulated in any combination of the above. For instance, you can make 20 calls and, even though you might get no appointments for that day, you will still accumulate 20 points. If you make a call and the prospect does not answer or call you back, you still get one point. The fact that you sourced the prospect's contact number and made the call deserves one point.

If you make a call for an appointment, and you succeed in setting a date and time, you will score those two points.

Regarding the four points for attempting to close, you will get them only if you try to close at least three times. Otherwise, score yourself three points.

The bottom line is not to quit work until you get 20 points every working day. You will then notice the amazing results.

There have been variations of the 20-Point Plan, with some advisors increasing it to a minimum of 25 or 30 points. I knew a top producer who ensured he got 30 points by lunch time. This is for each individual to decide. This system can also be adapted to work equally well in a number of other industries.

Winning

The first thing many successful agents are likely to worry about is being Number 1. Our culture is obsessed with winning. Winning is everything. If you are not Number 1, so the convention goes, you are nothing.

Wouldn't you agree that this is absolutely nonsensical?

If that were true, the majority of us would spend most of our lives being nothing. It is not possible to be Number 1 at anything for very long. Nor is it necessary. You do not have to be better than everybody else to be good. You do not have to be superior to be superb. Just be the very best you can be.

In this regard, the powerful words delivered by Dr Martin Luther King Jr. at the First Annual Institute on Non-violence and Social Change on 3 December 1956 in Montgomery, Alabama, is most appropriate.

"Whatever your life's work is, do it well. Even if it does not fall into the category of one of the so-called big professions, do it well. As one college president said, 'A man should do his job so well that the living, the dead and the unborn could do it no better.'

"If it falls your lot to be a street sweeper, sweep streets like Michelangelo painted pictures, like Shakespeare wrote poetry, like Beethoven composed music; sweep streets so well that all the hosts of Heaven and Earth will have to pause and say, 'Here lived a great street sweeper, who swept his job well.'"

As Douglas Malloch says:

> "If you can't be a pine on the top of the hill
> Be a scrub in the valley - but be
> The best little scrub by the side of the hill,

Be a bush if you can't be a tree.
If you can't be a highway, just be a trail.
If you can't be the sun, be a star.
It isn't by size that you win or fail -
Be the best of whatever you are."

That's all anyone can ever ask, or expect, of you... and that's all you should ever expect of others - particularly those close to you - and yourself. The question though is: are you performing at your optimal potential? Think about that for a while. If not, why not? Do you even know what your full capabilities really are? You, in turn, must give your 100% to anything you do. Demand more of yourself than anyone else does. Realise your full God-given potential.

Every one of you is special. Every one of you is unique. There is no other individual on Earth who is identical to you. Each and every one of you has the inherent potential to achieve greatness.

I repeat, all readers in the financial services industry who are not yet MDRT members should make a concerted effort and commitment to not only qualify for MDRT membership, but, more importantly, to attend an MDRT Annual Meeting.

It will signal a turning point in your career and your life. It is, without doubt, the greatest show on Earth. It will expand your horizon and demonstrate how you can reach levels of performance in your business, personal and family life that you never before dreamt possible.

The following profound poem encapsulates how we can incorporate true meaning and spirituality into our daily lives.

ABOU BEN ADHEM

Abou Ben Adhem! (May his tribe increase!)
Awoke one night from a deep dream of peace,
And saw, within the moonlight in his room,
Making it rich, and like a lily in bloom,
An angel writing in a book of gold —

Exceeding peace had made Ben Adhem bold,
And to the Presence in the room he said,
"What writest thou?"— The vision raised its head,
And with a look made of all sweet accord,
Answered, "The names of those who love the Lord."
"And is mine one?" said Abou. "Nay, not so,"
Replied the angel. Abou spoke more low,
But cheerly still, and said, "I pray thee, then,
Write me as one that loves his fellow men."

The angel wrote, and vanished. The next night,
It came again with a great wakening light,
And showed the names whom love of God had blessed,
And lo! Ben Adhem's name led all the rest.

- JAMES HENRY LEIGH HUNT

SIX

BALANCE IN LIFE: THE WHOLE PERSON CONCEPT

"Getting in balance is not so much about adopting new strategies to change your behaviours, as it is about realigning yourself in all of your thoughts so as to create a balance between what you desire and how you conduct your life on a daily basis."

— Wayne Dyer

People tend to be happier and more productive when all areas of life are balanced. What if someone said to you, "Tomorrow, I'm going to deposit $86, 400 into your bank account. You can spend as much as you want to tomorrow, but, at the end of the day, I'm going to take away any balance that remains and you'll never get another chance to spend it." How would you spend tomorrow? It's obvious that not a cent would remain at the end of the day.

This is what will happen to you and to me and to everybody else, tomorrow. However, it will not be dollars that we're spending; instead, it will be seconds. Every one of us will get 86, 400 seconds and we can spend them any way we want; we have to make sure we use every second to meet our goals in all areas of our lives.

"Guard well your spare moments. They are like uncut diamonds. Discard them and their value will never be known. Improve them and they will become the brightest gems in a useful life."

— **Ralph Waldo Emerson**

One of the basic tenets or doctrines of MDRT is the *Whole Person Concept* - creating success for your entire life, not just an isolated aspect of it. The Whole Person Concept highlights the fact that we need to ensure, at all times, that we lead a balanced life. It means having a balanced, systematic programme for growth and progress in the four broad areas of our lives: physical, emotional, intellectual and spiritual. Achieving a balanced lifestyle has many benefits, including peace of mind, increased productivity, and a sense of personal, professional, intellectual and spiritual fulfilment. Without this discipline, the body becomes weak, emotions uncontrolled, intellect absent and the spirit remains undeveloped.

To balance our lives, we must be proactive. This is the single most important investment we can ever make in life - investment in ourselves, in the only instrument we have with which to deal with life and to contribute to the upliftment of humanity.

The physical self is the body. We build its strength through regular exercise, proper nutrition, avoidance of harmful substances, adequate rest and sleep, chaste emotions and a healthy mental attitude. Unfortunately, a large part of humanity seems to think that external appearance - the clothes we wear, the right make-up, crash diets and so on - will fulfil our physical needs... but they don't. Instead, they lead to fleeting, temporary satisfaction. The greatest happiness occurs when we clearly understand that *'what is like poison in the beginning is like nectar in the end'* and *'what is like nectar in the beginning is like poison in the end'*. (*Bhagavad Gita*, Chapter XVIII, Verses 37 and 38.) Invariably, what seems pleasant at the beginning turns out unpleasant in the end and *vice versa*. We need to be wary of indulging in likes and dislikes, doing things merely because we like to, and not doing things that we should do (which we dislike), even though this might be beneficial in the long run. Think about this! How many of us 'like' to get up at 4:00 a.m. every morning to study and then exercise in a gym or outdoors? Or would we prefer to sleep at that hour? How many 'like' junk food? What are the consequences of prolonged periods of not exercising and eating junk food?

In respect of our emotional needs, the reality is that quality relationships are built on eternal values such as love, mutual respect, caring, compassion, sacrifice, responsibility and trust. Every person has a basic nature – characteristics, inclinations, behaviours that make them what they are. Properly assessing others and understanding their nature is one of the keys to successful relationships. It also encompasses keeping good company with people who uplift and affirm you for who you are, and entertaining noble emotions. In the wise words of Epictetus *"The key is to keep company only with people who uplift you, whose presence calls forth your best."*

We exercise our intellectual self through learning - through reading, writing, challenging, questioning everything, never taking anything for granted, conceiving virtuous, righteous thoughts and taking time to think and reason. It is incumbent on all of us to engage in life-long learning and growth. The greatest investment we can make is to invest in ourselves - our personal growth and development.

We exercise our spiritual self through reading literature that inspires us, through study and reflection, contemplation on the higher values in life, and spending time in natural environments. We do this by changing our focus from external pursuits to the higher Self within.

> "This above all - to thine own self be true; and it must follow, as the night the day, thou canst not be false to any man."

> **— From Hamlet by William Shakespeare.**

The Million Dollar Round Table has a systematic approach to the Whole Person Concept. While the four broad categories are mentioned above, MDRT expands on these concepts.

The following is an extract from MDRT's brochure, 'The Whole Person – Creating Success for Your Entire Life'.

DEFINING THE WHOLE PERSON

Becoming a Whole Person is not a one-time event. Whole Persons are engaged in a lifetime quest to achieve balance in all aspects of their lives. Achieving one's full potential, while engaging in a meaningful and rewarding journey, is a lifelong goal.

RELATIONSHIPS Whole Persons spend meaningful time with their spouses, children, immediate family and friends. They strive to make sharing, love, mutual respect and openness the cornerstones of these relationships.

HEALTH Whole Persons maintain a sound mind and body through study, a well-balanced diet, regular exercise, and lifestyle choices conducive to physical and mental well-being.

EDUCATION Whole Persons seek to enrich their lives through continual intellectual development. They enthusiastically engage in meaningful pursuits that enrich their lives and the lives of others.

CAREER Whole Persons strive to become more productive, enhance their professional esteem, pursue increased knowledge, and contribute to industry and professional organizations. They also seek to improve the careers of fellow professionals through mentorship and leading by example.

SERVICE Whole Persons contribute "hands-on" time, including energy and leadership, and financial resources to community organizations, educational institutions, government, civic and charitable organizations, and other worthwhile endeavors, voluntarily and without expectation of personal gain.

FINANCIAL Whole Persons know how to live within their means, to enjoy and share the fruits of their labor, and to plan and implement programs for the creation, accumulation and preservation of capital consistent with the stages of their lives.

SPIRITUAL Whole Persons live their lives according to their faith and strive to grow spiritually while helping others toward greater fulfillment.

FROM THE EXECUTIVE COMMITTEE

When philosopher Dr. Mortimer J. Adler introduced MDRT members to the Whole Person concept at the 1961 Annual Meeting, little did he know the full impact his words would have on the lives of so many people more than four decades later.

At MDRT, we are committed to this vitally important concept, and want all our members to understand the value and benefits of balancing their lives in seven critical areas: relationships, health, education, career, service, financial and spiritual. In fact, in light of today's tough economic climate, committing to be a Whole Person has perhaps never been more important.

Visit www.mdrt.org to learn more about several exciting Whole Person initiatives that will help our members create success for their entire life. We hope you will engage in these activities and commit to being a Whole Person this year and for years to come.

MDRT Executive Committee

MDRT
The Premier
Association of Financial
Professionals ®

Million Dollar Round Table
325 West Touhy Avenue
Park Ridge, IL 60068 USA

Phone: +1 847.692.6378
Fax: +1 847.518.8921
Web site: www.mdrt.org

The **Whole Person**

Creating Success for Your Entire Life

STAYING IN BALANCE DAY AFTER DAY

For some people, achieving a good work-life balance seems to come naturally. Yet, many of us constantly struggle to manage priorities in our professional and personal lives.

As a successful financial services professional, are you leading the fulfilling and enriching life that you want? Or, do you recognize there are areas you may be neglecting or could improve?

With all the demands for your time and attention, it is easy to lose touch with the other equally important aspects of your life—family, community service, health and spirituality. To bring all those elements into balance, many MDRT members have embraced the Whole Person concept.

Living a well-rounded, balanced lifestyle and becoming a Whole Person is the foundation for:

- Ongoing happiness
- Good health
- Loving family relationships
- Financial security
- Strong friendships
- Intellectual fulfillment
- Self-confidence

THE BALANCE QUIZ

To highlight imbalances in your life that may require attention, review each statement and assess yourself on a scale of 1 (low) to 10 (high). Add your scores for each category and enter the total next to the category heading. Maximum score per category is 30.

RELATIONSHIPS   Total score ___
___ a. Spending time with my family and friends is structured in my daily and weekly schedule.
___ b. I give family and friends my full attention by turning off my phone/PDA/BlackBerry/laptop/iPod when I am with them.
___ c. I regularly talk with family members and ask how I can be a more loving spouse/parent/etc.

HEALTH   Total score ___
___ a. I invest at least 30 minutes in cardiovascular exercise three times per week.
___ b. Meals are well balanced and I exercise moderation in sweets and other snacks.
___ c. I choose a smoke-free life and control alcoholic consumption.

EDUCATION   Total score ___
___ a. Reading, studying and attending classes (traditional or virtual) is important to me.
___ b. I have a passion for learning.
___ c. Electronic entertainment (Internet, television, movies) is used in moderation.

CAREER   Total score ___
___ a. I invest time and other resources in the development of my intellectual resources.
___ b. Increasing productivity is a component of my personal and professional development plan.
___ c. I have created and regularly review my business and succession plan.

SERVICE   Total score ___
___ a. I am actively engaged in community or industry service activities.
___ b. Others in the community view me as a leader and can count on my help when needed.
___ c. I positively influence the lives of others through formal or informal mentorship.

FINANCIAL   Total score ___
___ a. I have written financial goals.
___ b. I live within my income.
___ c. I am creating, accumulating and preserving capital consistent with my stage in life.

SPIRITUAL   Total score ___
___ a. I have strong personal spiritual beliefs.
___ b. I spend time each day reflecting or reading spiritually inspiring materials.
___ c. I am passionate about leading a life that reflects my strong personal values.

Now, transfer your scores to the rings on the diagram. Then, connect the marks from one category to another.

Review the resulting form, shape and location. If your scores are fairly consistent, they form an approximate circle and fall mainly in the outer green ring—congratulations, you are living a well balanced life!

If, however, your scores vary significantly, form several peaks and valleys, or fall consistently near the inner brown ring, don't be surprised; most people who take this quiz find some areas of their lives that are out of balance.

Look closely at your highest and lowest scores; they are a reflection of your current priorities. If the resulting imbalance revealed on the diagram concerns you, take steps today to create a better balance in your life. For example, you may want to consider joining a study group, volunteering, going back to school, developing a hobby, getting more exercise, etc.

Remember, we are all on a journey to reach our full human potential.

It's time to get involved in your whole life again. Where would you like to grow?

- Relationships
- Service
- Health
- Financial
- Education
- Spiritual
- Career

THE WHOLE PERSON - Creating Success for Your Entire Life

STAYING IN BALANCE DAY AFTER DAY

For some people, achieving a good work-life balance seems to come naturally. Yet, many of us constantly struggle to manage priorities in our professional and personal lives.

As a successful financial services professional, are you leading the fulfilling and enriching life that you want? Or, do you recognise that there are areas you might be neglecting or could improve?

With all the demands for your time and attention, it is easy to lose touch with the other equally important aspects of your life - family, community service, health and spirituality. To bring all those elements into balance, many MDRT members have embraced the Whole Person Concept.

Living a well-rounded, balanced lifestyle and becoming a whole person is the foundation for:

- Ongoing happiness.

- Loving family relationships.

- Strong friendships.

- Self-confidence.

- Good health.

- Financial security.

- Emotional maturity.

- Intellectual fulfilment.

FROM THE MDRT EXECUTIVE COMMITTEE

When philosopher Dr Mortimer J Adler introduced MDRT members to the Whole Person Concept at the 1961 Annual Meeting, little did he know the full impact his words would have on the lives of so many people decades later.

At MDRT, we are committed to this vitally important concept, and we want all our members to understand the value and benefits of balancing their lives in seven critical areas: relationships, health, education, career, service, financial and spiritual. In fact, in light of today's tough economic climate, committing to be a whole person has perhaps never been more important.

Visit http://www.mdrt.org to learn more about several exciting Whole Person initiatives that will help our members create success for their entire life. We hope you will engage in these activities and commit to being a whole person this year and for years to come.

DEFINING THE WHOLE PERSON

Becoming a Whole Person is not a one-time event. Whole Persons are engaged in a lifetime quest to achieve balance in all aspects of their lives. Achieving one's full potential, while engaging in a meaningful and rewarding journey, is a lifelong goal.

RELATIONSHIPS: Whole persons spend meaningful time with their spouses, children, immediate family and friends. They strive to make sharing, love, mutual respect and openness the cornerstones of these relationships.

HEALTH: Whole persons maintain a sound mind and body through study, a well-balanced diet, regular exercise, and lifestyle choices conducive to physical and mental wellbeing.

EDUCATION: Whole persons seek to enrich their lives through continual intellectual development. They enthusiastically engage in meaningful pursuits that enrich their lives and the lives of others.

CAREER: Whole persons strive to become more productive, enhance their professional esteem, pursue increased knowledge, and contribute to industry and professional organisations. They also seek to improve the careers of fellow professionals through mentorship and leading by example.

SERVICE: Whole persons contribute 'hands-on' time - including energy and leadership, and financial resources - to community organisations, educational institutions, government, civic and charitable organisations, and other worthwhile endeavours, voluntarily and without expectation of personal gain.

FINANCIAL: Whole persons know how to live within their means, to enjoy and share the fruits of their labour, and to plan and implement programmes for the creation, accumulation and preservation of capital consistent with the stages of their lives.

SPIRITUAL: Whole persons live their lives according to their faith and strive to grow spiritually while helping others toward greater fulfilment.

THE BALANCE QUIZ

Take *The Balance Quiz* – see extracts from the MDRT brochure below. Draw it as indicated.

To highlight imbalances in your life that might require attention, review each statement below and assess yourself on a scale of 1 (low) to 10 (high). Draw a large circle, like a bicycle wheel with spokes. Draw another smaller circle and a third even smaller - all an equal distance apart. The big circle should thus be divided into three circles, the outer (colour this green), the middle (colour orange) and the inner, around the centre (colour brown). At the edge of each circle, write in 10, 20 and 30 from the edge of the inner, middle and outer circles respectively. Add straight lines from the centre of the circle to the circumference. Label each line, as per the seven areas listed below, which comprise the whole person. Add your scores for each category and enter the total next to the category heading. Maximum score per category is 30, 10 for each of the three sub-sections.

RELATIONSHIPS: Total score _____

_____ a. Spending time with my family and friends is structured in my daily and weekly schedule.

_____ b. I give family and friends my full attention by turning off my phone/laptop/iPad or other electronic equipment when I am with them.

_____ c. I regularly talk with family members and ask how I can be a more loving spouse/parent/etc.

HEALTH: Total score _____

_____ a. I invest at least 30 minutes in cardiovascular exercise three times per week.

_____ b. Meals are well balanced and I exercise moderation in sweets and other snacks.

_____ c. I choose a smoke-free life and control alcoholic consumption.

EDUCATION: Total score _____

_____ a. Reading, studying and attending classes (traditional or virtual) is important to me.

_____ b. I have a passion for learning.

_____ c. Electronic entertainment (Internet, television, movies) is used in moderation.

CAREER: Total score _____

_____ a. I invest time and other resources in the development of my intellectual resources.

_____ b. Increasing productivity is a component of my personal and professional development plan.

_____ c. I have created and regularly review my business and succession plan.

SERVICE: Total score _____

_____ a. I am actively engaged in community or industry service activities.

_____ b. Others in the community view me as a leader and can count on my help when needed.

_____ c. I positively influence the lives of others through formal or informal mentorship.

FINANCIAL: Total score _____

_____ a. I have written financial goals.

_____ b. I live within my income.

_____ c. I am creating, accumulating and preserving capital consistent with my stage in life.

SPIRITUAL: Total score _____

_____ a. I have strong personal spiritual beliefs.

_____ b. I spend time each day reflecting or reading spiritually inspiring materials.

_____ c. I am passionate about leading a life that reflects my strong personal values.

Now, transfer your scores to the rings on the diagram.

Then, connect the marks from one category to another.

Review the resulting form, shape and location.

If your scores are fairly consistent, they form an approximate circle and fall mainly in the outer green ring - congratulations, you are living a well-balanced life!

If, however, your scores vary significantly, form several peaks and valleys, or fall consistently near the inner brown ring, don't be surprised; most people who take this quiz find some areas of their lives that are out of balance.

Look closely at your highest and lowest scores; they are a reflection of your current priorities. If the resulting imbalance revealed on the diagram concerns you, take steps today to create a better balance in your life. For example, you might want to consider joining a study group, volunteering, going back to school, developing a hobby or getting more exercise, etc.

Remember, we are all on a journey to reach our full human potential.

It's time to get involved in your whole life again.

Where would you like to grow?

Relationships | Health | Education | Career | Service | Financial | Spiritual

"When I let go of what I am,
I become what I might be."

— George Bernard Shaw

The late Steven Covey stated that one of the most powerful methods to cultivate the passion of vision is to create and live by a mission statement, philosophy or creed. Such statements capture what you want to be and do - what qualities you want to develop, what you want to accomplish and what contributions you want to make. Clarity on these issues is critical, because it affects everything else - the goals you set, the decisions you make, the paradigms you hold and the way you spend your time.

Create a personal mission statement if you do not already have one. This personal mission statement, based on correct principles, becomes your individual standard. It is your personal constitution, an ideal, the basis from which you make life-directing and daily decisions in the midst of the circumstances and emotions that affect your life.

Don't become overwhelmed by the task of writing a personal mission statement or the need to make it perfect. Instead, write a rough draft and then work to refine it over the next several weeks or months. Because each individual is unique, a personal mission statement will reflect that uniqueness, both in content and form. An effective mission statement can consist of a few words or several pages. To be empowering, it has to become a living, breathing document. You must ponder it, memorise it, review it and update it. Write your personal mission statement into your heart and mind.

"Whoever does not regard what he has as most ample wealth,
Is unhappy, though he be master of the world."

— Epictetus

What follows demonstrates the potential impact MDRT can have on our family and all those we contact.

My eldest daughter, Sarisha, who was in grade 10 in 1996, did one of her Maris Stella High school projects on MDRT, with numerous slides extracted from MDRT's website, including MDRT's Purpose, History, Foundation, Member Benefits, Code of Ethics, Annual Meeting, etc. She screened the video "Gifted Hands" by Benjamin Carson and included his story, as well as a summary of the presentation "Random Acts of Kindness" by Charles C Wall Ph.D., in the project. She presented this to her teachers and fellow class students. Following are a few extracts from her 21-page project:

"MDRT is an organization that portrays messages that are universally applicable. They apply to all people in all spheres of life, not only people working in the insurance industry. The MDRT Annual Meeting is a very unique gathering. It is one of its kind. It is the insurance industry's sales meeting 'par excellence'. Here the world's leading advisers gather in a spirit of sharing and camaraderie that is unrivalled in the world of commerce. It can change lives. It can create new heroes."

"The main reason I chose to do my project on MDRT is because I wanted to share some wonderful things from the MDRT speakers. When my father comes back from an MDRT Annual Meeting, his whole spirit is uplifted and he comes back really motivated and excited to achieve things in life. The cause of all his exuberance is because of the grand speakers that address him at the Annual Meeting. He brings back audio and visual tapes of speakers and also books and written speeches. By reading some of these and watching and listening to tapes, I have also been touched by various speakers. I am going to tell you about two speakers I found most excellent. They are Dr. Benjamin Carson and Professor Charles Wall."

She then read to the class extracts from my presentation on Visualization (Chapter 3) and proceeded to share Benjamin Carson's story (Chapter 13), followed by Prof. Charles Wall's story, with a big poster containing his main message:

"TODAY I WILL COMMIT ONE RANDON ACT OF KINDNESS - WILL YOU?"

Sarisha showed the Benjamin Carson Video and concluded her presentation with the words:

"MDRT is a superb organization. By doing this project I am glad I have made you aware of its existence. MDRT membership continues to grow internationally."

Her teacher commented: "Not only have you made us aware - you have inspired us!"

The following extracts from her teacher's report demonstrate how far and wide MDRT's impact spreads.

"Your project was beautifully, and professionally presented and could easily be used at post-school level.

I particularly enjoy seeing pupils being directly motivated by their parent's success, which was so evident in your project.

What you did though was to take this a step further and inspire and motivate your teachers and the rest of the class by your excellent, thoughtful and sincere oral presentation. Thank you for taking the time to present such quality work, and for showing us such an appropriate video which summed up your address so well.

Excellent work!"

Her teacher, Ms M. Roberts, gave her an A+ for this project.

It is incumbent on members who attend an MDRT Annual Meeting to share the wisdom and inspirational content you experience at the meeting, as well as DVDs of Main Platform presentations, with your family, friends, community, affiliate associations, etc. Spread the message to help uplift humanity. This is what I did after every meeting and also gave feedback at seminars held by the Life Underwriters Association virtually every year. This will also help you further balance your lives.

> "If you would learn the secret of right relations, look only for the divine in people and things, and leave all the rest to God."
>
> — J. Allen Boone

What a wonderful world we'd have if everyone did this.

The Turkey and the Ant

The following brilliant poem/fable by John Gay highlights the human weakness of finding faults in others while totally ignoring our own flaws, although they may be far greater. In this fable, the turkey was destroying thousands of ants for her breakfast but complaining of man killing a turkey for Christmas. Part of living a balanced life is to entertain noble thoughts, have a friendly disposition, be grateful for what we have and treat all beings with fairness and dignity.

In other men we faults can spy,
And blame the mote that dims their eye,
Each little speck and blemish find,
To our own stronger errors blind.

A Turkey, tir'd of common food,
Forsook the barn, and sought the wood,

Behind her ran her infant train,
Collecting here and there a grain.

Draw near, my birds, the mother cries,
This hill delicious fare supplies;
Behold, the busy Negro race,
See, millions blacken all the place!

Fear not. Like me, with freedom eat;
An ant is most delightful meat.
How blest, how envy'd were our life,
Could we but 'scape the poult'rer's knife!
But man, curst man on turkey preys,
And Christmas shortens all our days;
Sometimes with oysters we combine,
Sometimes assist the sav'ry chine.

From the low peasant to the lord,
The turkey smoaks on ev'ry board.
Sure men for gluttony are curst,
Of the sev'n deadly sins the worst.

An Ant, who climb'd beyond his reach,
Thus answer'd from the neighb'ring beech.
Ere you remark another's sin.
Bid thy own conscience look within.
Control thy more voracious bill,
Nor for a breakfast nations kill.

- JOHN GAY

"I believe that the first test of a great man is his humility. I don't mean
by humility, doubt of his power. But really great men have a curious
feeling that the greatness is not of them, but through them. And they
see something divine in every other man and are endlessly, foolishly,
incredibly merciful."

— John Ruskin

SEVEN

LIFE IN PERSPECTIVE

"Your time is limited, so don't waste it living someone else's life. Don't be trapped by dogma - which is living with the results of other people's thinking. Don't let the noise of others' opinions drown out your own inner voice. And, most important, have the courage to follow your heart and intuition."

— Steve Jobs

The 1989 MDRT Annual Meeting in Toronto, Canada was amazing! The selection of dynamic main platform speakers was unbelievable. In this chapter, I want to focus on one of the powerful main platform presentations by Dr Ivan Fitzwater.

Before you read the rest of this, and in order to get maximum value from his presentation, write down your 10 top priorities, in order of importance i.e. the most important being number one, proceeding to the second most important, and so forth.

Exercise

List your top 10 current priorities.

1. _____

2. _____

3. _____

4. _____

5. _____

6. _____

7. _____

8. _____

9. _____

10. _____

We'll come back to this list later. If you have not yet listed your top 10 priorities, please do so now.

> "The Moving Finger writes; and, having writ,
> Moves on: nor all thy Piety nor Wit
> Shall lure it back to cancel half a Line,
> Nor all thy Tears wash out a Word of it."
>
> — Omar Khayyam

Dr Ivan Fitzwater is a 'time and stress management' expert who gave us ten ideas that changed his life; ten ideas that rescued him from workaholism and an early death.

Not all of them will be new to you, but, when conscientiously applied, they will increase your productivity by helping you to work smarter, not harder.

1. Plan

Start every day by making a list of the things that you must get done that day. Not a list of all the things that you would *like* to do, as that list becomes too long and it's self-defeating. Rather, list the things that *must* be done. Then, put a check beside the one on the list that's most important and start on that item. Here's a suggestion that will really payoff: do one thing at a time from beginning to end and never work on two things at the same time. If there's anything on your list that you must do, but really dread doing, do it first and get it out of the way, or the thought of it will ruin your whole day.

2. Delegate

Never do anything that anyone who works for you can do.

3. Maximise the telephone

When you go anywhere for any reason, ask yourself, *"Can I handle this by telephone?"* If the answer is *yes*, don't make the trip - telephone instead. Also, shorten your telephone calls and get right down to business. Have a set time in your daily schedule when you make all your outgoing calls.

4. Block interruptions

Make sure your secretary knows how to screen telephone calls for priority. When in the office, keep your door closed.

5. Make decisions

Many people suffer from a phenomenon called *'analysis paralysis'*. They are always analysing or reviewing, but they are never deciding. Identify the decisions that must be made in a given period of time and set a deadline for each.

6. Streamline your meetings

Whether you are conducting or attending a meeting, always insist that the meeting starts on time. Let people know, in advance, when the meeting will end, and never violate that.

7. Increase productivity by rewarding yourself

When we reward ourselves for high productivity, we tend to keep ourselves working at a high level of intensity. If I tell my family in the morning that I'll be home at 5 p.m., I find that I work hard all day to make this happy goal come true.

8. Work with a clean desk

Start every day with a clean desk and end every day with a clean desk - have only one task on the desk at any one time. This is probably the most important management suggestion ever made. Try this experiment: every time you pick up a piece of paper without getting rid of it, put a dot on it when you put it back down on your desk. Watch these papers catch 'chickenpox' as you interrupt yourself over and over again.

9. Avoid perfectionism

Don't work better than what is needed to get the job done. Use short cuts that don't diminish quality.

10. Keep life in perspective

Time is a unique resource. It's the only resource that we can't store, we can't borrow and we can't recycle. The only thing that we can do with time is spend it as it comes to us. This resource has to be used for all phases of life, not just work. Indeed, we do better work when we are using this unique resource in such a way that it brings stability and fulfilment to all parts of our lives. You might want to try this experiment, which is part of an activity that Dr Fritzwater employs in his time management seminar. Pretend that you have just learnt that you have exactly six months to live. However, the doctor says that you are going to have reasonably good health right to the last day. What would you do in the next six months? I think you will immediately find that areas other than work will come into proper balance. We suddenly realise time is a finite resource, so we start giving attention to the things that really matter, such as our family relationships, our spiritual life and our civic responsibility. Dr Fitzwater says that it is amazing how people's priorities suddenly change when faced with the prospect of impending death. Priorities that were previously 7, 8 and 9 on the list get elevated to numbers 1, 2 and 3.

> "True wisdom comes to each of us when we realize how little we understand about life, ourselves, and the world around us."
>
> — **Socrates**

In this regard, I quote some really profound words of wisdom from the book, *The Untethered Soul* by Michael A. Singer (Chapter 17 *"Contemplating Death"*)

"It shouldn't take death to challenge you to live at your highest level. Why wait until everything is taken from you before you learn to dig down deep inside yourself to reach your highest potential? A wise person affirms, "If with one breath all of this can change, then I want to live at the highest level while I'm alive. I'm going to stop bothering the people I love. I'm going to live life from the deepest part of my being."

He then talks about Consciousness, and says:

"This is the consciousness necessary for deep and meaningful relationships. Look how callous we get with our loved ones. We take it for granted that they're there and that they'll continue to be there for us. What if they died? What if you died? What if you know that this evening would be the last time you'd see them? Imagine that an angel comes down and tells you, *straighten up your affairs. You will not awake from your sleep tonight. You're coming to me.* Then you'd know that every person you see that day, you'd be seeing for the last time. How would you feel? How would you interact with them? Would you even bother with the little grudges and complaints you've been carrying around? How much love would you give the ones you love, knowing it would be the last time you'd get to be with them? Think about what it would be like if you lived like that every moment with everyone. Your life would be entirely different. You should contemplate this. Death is not a morbid thought. Death is the greatest teacher in all of life."

Michael Singer then implores us to examine where we put out time and energy, and says:

"Take a moment to look at the things you think you need. Look at how much time and energy you put into various activities. Imagine if you knew you were going to die within a week or a month. How would that change things? How would your priorities change? How would your thoughts change? Think honestly about what you would do with your last week. What a wonderful thought to contemplate. Then ponder this question: If that's really what you would do with your last week, what are you doing with the rest of your time? Wasting it? Throwing it away? Treating it like it's not something precious? What are you doing with life? That is what death asks you."

He then states emphatically that death is a great teacher, as follows:

"Death is a great teacher. But who lives with that level of awareness? It doesn't matter what age you are; at any time you could take a breath and there may never be another. It happens all the time – to babies, to teenagers, to people in mid-life – not just to the aged. One breath and they're gone. No one knows when their time will be. That's not how it works.

So why not be bold enough to regularly reflect on how you would live that last week?

You must not be afraid to discuss death. Don't get uptight about it. Instead, let this knowledge help you to live every moment of your life fully, because every moment matters. That's what happens when somebody knows they only have a week left. You can be certain that they would tell you that the most important week they ever had was that last week. Everything is a million times more meaningful in that final week. What if you were to live every week that way?"

Finally, Michael Singer asks why we aren't living that way, concluding this section with the words:

> "At this point you should ask yourself why you aren't living that way. You are going to die. You know that. You just don't know when. Every single thing will be taken from you. You will leave behind your possessions, your loved ones, and all your hopes and dreams for this life. You'll be taken right out from where you are. You'll no longer be able to fill the roles you were so busy playing. Death changes everything in a flash. That's the reality of the situation. If all these things can be changed in an instant, then maybe they aren't so real after all. Maybe you'd better check out who you are. Maybe you should look deeper.
>
> The beauty of embracing deep truths is that you don't have to change your life; you just change how you live your life. It's not what you're doing; it's how much of you is doing it.
>
> Learn to live as though you are facing death at all times, and you'll become bolder and more open. If you live life fully, you won't have any last wishes. You will have lived them every moment."

> — **Michael A. Singer, The Untethered Soul: The Journey Beyond Yourself**

Dr Fitzwater quoted the case of a young attorney who came up to him at the end of one of his time management seminars and stated that the 'six months to live' exercise was particularly revealing to him. He said, "I have a little girl of three and a little boy of five, and I have been so busy going to law school and getting my practice underway that I hardly know either of them. Starting next week, I'm going to schedule time with them."

Unfortunately, on the way home from the seminar that afternoon, his car hydroplaned on the wet pavement and he hit a tree and was killed. His time had run out!

The question is: **are you going to wait for your time to run out before you realise what the most important priorities in your life are?**

Reflect on this for a few moments.

> "Your days are numbered. Use them to throw open the windows of your soul to the sun. If you do not, the sun will soon set, and you with it."

> — **Marcus Aurelius**

Exercise

Without referring to the first list of priorities you entered above, now list 10 things that you would prioritise if you just learnt that you have only six months more to live.

1. _____

2. _____

3. _____

4. _____

5. _____

6. _____

7. _____

8. _____

9. _____

10. _____

Please don't proceed on to the next chapter until you have listed the 10 most important things to do if you had just six months left to live.

> "Things which matter most must never be at the mercy of things which matter least."
>
> — Johann Wolfgang von Goethe

The following beautiful poem by British Nobel laureate Rudyard Kipling, written in the form of paternal advice to the poet's son, reminds us to keep a proper perspective of life.

If—BY RUDYARD KIPLING

If you can keep your head when all about you
Are losing theirs and blaming it on you;
If you can trust yourself when all men doubt you,
But make allowance for their doubting too;
If you can wait and not be tired by waiting,
Or being lied about, don't deal in lies,

Or being hated, don't give way to hating,
And yet don't look too good, nor talk too wise:

If you can dream - and not make dreams your master;
If you can think - and not make thoughts your aim;
If you can meet with Triumph and Disaster
And treat those two impostors just the same;
If you can bear to hear the truth you've spoken
Twisted by knaves to make a trap for fools,
Or watch the things you gave your life to, broken,
And stoop and build 'em up with worn-out tools:

If you can make one heap of all your winnings
And risk it on one turn of pitch-and-toss,
And lose, and start again at your beginnings
And never breathe a word about your loss;
If you can force your heart and nerve and sinew
To serve your turn long after they are gone,
And so hold on when there is nothing in you
Except the Will which says to them: 'Hold on!'

If you can talk with crowds and keep your virtue,
Or walk with kings - nor lose the common touch,
If neither foes nor loving friends can hurt you,
If all men count with you, but none too much;
If you can fill the unforgiving minute
With sixty seconds' worth of distance run,
Yours is the Earth and everything that's in it,
And - which is more - you'll be a man, my son!

RUDYARD KIPLING

"Be happy for this moment. This moment is your life."

— Omar Khayyam

EIGHT

MOULDERS OF DREAMS

"We are responsible for what we are, and whatever we wish ourselves to be, we have the power to make ourselves. If what we are now has been the result of our own past actions, it certainly follows that whatever we wish to be in future can be produced by our present actions; so we have to know how to act."

— **Swami Vivekananda**

In one of the most memorable talks of the 1989 MDRT Annual Meeting, **GUY RICE DOUD** spoke on 'Moulders of Dreams'. He was voted national 'Teacher of the Year' in the USA in 1986. He stated that a poll of kindergarten children revealed that 96% of them felt good about themselves; that is, they felt good about who they are. A poll of seniors, on the other hand, indicated that only about 6% are happy with themselves. What happens to their self-esteem? What happens to the self-confidence reflected in the eyes of the little kids as they grow up? What takes away those smiles?

He asks, "What happens between kindergarten and the time we are ready to enter the world?" A lot happens... and what happens has affected where we are today. It happens through what he calls the 'hidden curriculum' - the negative input that we receive that teaches us where we fit in, what our values are and whether or not we have any potential.

Guy said that he had a very hard life and would have been just another school dropout, another statistic, had it not been for the fact that somebody cared. That 'somebody' was his teachers. As a teacher, he has come to believe that, no matter what profession you are in, people won't care how much you know until they know how much you care.

He went on, and I quote: "If it hadn't been for those teachers who cared, I don't know where I'd be today. But how did people handle these feelings of low self-esteem? Some of them aren't fortunate enough to find those people who really care. So I see kids today who are searching, searching. You know what these kids grow up to be as adults? They are searching for the answers. They have turned to drugs, and they have turned to sex and they have turned to trying to acquire materialistic possessions in an attempt to give them meaning and purpose in life. And it's fruitless and it's empty."

"Some people become workaholics. And this searching continues on into adulthood, and mixed-up, insecure kids become mixed-up, insecure adults. But as adults we're better at 'wearing the masks'. Pretending is an art that has become second nature with us. We give the impression that we're secure, that all is sunny and unruffled with us, within as well as without, that confidence is our name, coolness is our game, that we're in charge and that we need no one."

Guy stated that he's come to believe that, and I quote: "Unless you have learnt to love and to be loved, learnt to be honest and open, learnt to share your dreams and your hurts, you've never really learnt to live.

The greatest tragedy of life is to suddenly realise that you've only been filling space."

One of Guy's heroes is the Apostle Paul. Paul wrote a letter to a church in Corinth in which he said: "Your life is a letter being read by everybody; it's a letter. And it's a letter that's not written in ink. And it's a letter that's not written in stone. But it's a letter that's written on the tablet of the human heart."

> "It is the beauty within us that makes it possible for us to recognize the beauty around us. The question is not what you look at but what you see."
>
> — Henry David Thoreau

Guy went on: "Our lives are letters. You are a teacher. Parents are the greatest teachers of all. We are teachers; we're teaching everybody every day by the lives that we live. We are part of this whole process that we call the human race."

In April 1986, Guy had the honour of being invited into the Oval Office to meet with the President of the US - Ronald Reagan. The president read out to Guy a poem that he'd come across many years ago, about the importance of teachers. It was by a journalist, Clark Mollenhoff, and it went as follows:

"Teachers. You are the moulders of their dreams. The gods who build or crush their young beliefs of right or wrong. You are the spark that sets a flame on the poet's hand and lights the flame of some great singer's song. You are the God of the young, the very young. You are the guardian of a million dreams. Your every smile or frown can heal or pierce a heart. Yours are a hundred lives, a thousand lives. Yours, the pride of loving them, the sorrow, too. Your patient work, your touch, make you the gods of hope who fill their soul with dreams to make those dreams come true."

Guy closed his remarkable talk by stating: "Moulders of dreams, that's what we all are. Our lives can either make or break somebody else. I've seen kids who so desperately need love. And I've seen adults who desperately need love."

Accept your calling to be a 'moulder of dreams'. Realise that your life is a letter. Begin moulding at home. Make sure that everything that needs saying has been said. Make sure that everything that needs doing has been done. Drop everything else and make sure that your home is in order. Then realise your commitment to your fellow man.

Someone has said that there are two types of people in the world: 'life-orientated' and 'death-orientated'. Death-orientated people take a look at life and say, *"Well, this is the way it is; guess I can't do much about it."* Life-orientated people take a look at life and see it as they would like it to be, and realise that they can make it happen. They can! Be a life-orientated person, dear friend. And remember: **No one will ever care how much you know, until they know how much you care!**

"Whatever you do, you need courage. Whatever course you decide upon, there is always someone to tell you that you are wrong. There are always difficulties arising that tempt you to believe your critics are right. To map out a course of action and follow it to an end requires some of the same courage that a soldier needs. Peace has its victories, but it takes brave men and women to win them."

— **Ralph Waldo Emerson**

NINE

SUCCESS IS A JOURNEY

"Twenty years from now, you will be more disappointed by the things that you didn't do than by the ones you did do. So throw off the bowlines. Sail away from the safe harbour. Catch the trade winds in your sails. Explore. Dream. Discover."

— **Mark Twain**

I t was such a privilege to hear **BRIAN TRACY**, best-selling author, entrepreneur and success expert, speak from the main platform at an MDRT Annual Meeting on the subject 'success is a journey'.

At the age of 20, together with a few friends, Brian undertook to travel from Vancouver, Canada, to Johannesburg, South Africa. They encountered one problem after the other, running out of money over and over, and straining every muscle of their bodies trying to ride bicycles across France and Spain. Their Land Rover broke down again and again. They suffered from dysentery, heat stroke and exhaustion. Then they had to cross the Sahara Desert, the largest desert in the world, which stretches 5, 000 miles from the Atlantic Ocean to the Red Sea, and measures 800 miles in length. Over 1, 300 people had perished in that stretch over the last 20 years. Forty-two vehicles had broken down in the desert and many of their drivers were never seen again. Most people they came across thought they were mad to attempt such a crossing. Everywhere they went, people told them that they would die in the desert.

"The price of anything is the amount of life you exchange for it."

— Henry David Thoreau

Brian said he learnt a valuable lesson - whenever you try to do something out of the ordinary, people will line up to tell you that you can't do it, why you can't do it, that you will lose your time, lose your money, that you will, in effect, 'die in the desert'. Even people who should know better will try to discourage you. However, to achieve anything great or worthwhile, you must train yourself to rise above these people, ignoring them. One of his friends pulled out before the Sahara crossing. Just Brian and another friend were left. Ultimately, 12 months after leaving Vancouver, having crossed three continents and travelling 17, 000 miles, they eventually made it to the southern tip of Africa.

"The people who get on in this world are the people who get up and look for the circumstances they want, and, if they can't find them, make them."

— George Bernard Shaw

Brian closed his talk by sharing what he learnt about life and success in the Sahara crossing. He gave seven rules you can apply to any challenge you face in achieving anything you desire.

RULE 1: The most important key to achieving great success is to decide on your goal and then: *launch. Get started. Take action.* A 12-year study at Boston College concluded that the act of taking the first step is what separates winners from losers.

RULE 2: Once you have launched, like a guided missile towards your goal, never consider the possibility of failure. The Germans have a saying: *"Always forward, never backward."*

RULE 3: The biggest goal in the world can be accomplished if you just take it *one step at a time.* Winston Churchill once said: *"Our business is not to see what lies dimly at a distance, but to do what lies clearly at hand."* The only time you will ever have is now; you will be on your way to making a great life.

RULE 4: Watch out for the naysayers, the negative people around you who are always telling you that: *"You'll die in the desert."* Seek the company of positive people - winners. *Fly with the eagles* and refuse to listen to objections and reasons you can't succeed. Someone once said that if every possible objection must first be overcome, nothing will ever get done.

> "If I can't make it through one door, I'll go through another door - or I'll make a door. Something terrific will come no matter how dark the present."
>
> — **Rabindranath Tagore**

RULE 5: *Welcome obstacles and difficulties* as valuable and inevitable steps on the ladder of success. Remember that difficulties come not to obstruct, but to instruct. When you look back on any achievement, you will find that it was preceded by many difficulties. They are the price that you pay for success.

RULE 6: Be *clear* about your goal and be *flexible* about the process of achieving it. Be willing to change to try something new. Keep your mind open, fluid and flexible. Remember, it's not what you have, but what you do with what you have that separates winners from losers. It isn't what happens to you, but how you respond to what happens to you that counts. In the final analysis, your response to the adversity of life is the real measure of who you are. The Greek philosopher, Epictetus, said, *"Circumstances do not make the man; they merely reveal him to himself."* Finally,

RULE 7: Remember, *no one does it alone.* When life is over, it will be the people we lived and laughed and loved with who we remember more than anything else.

Don't be afraid to ask for help from others. It's a mark of strength, courage and character. Don't be reluctant to give of yourself to others generously. It's the mark of caring, compassion and personal greatness.

"For it is in giving that we receive."

— St. Francis of Assisi

After the Sahara crossing, Brian was assured that he could accomplish anything that he set his mind to do. He felt programmed for success in life.

Brian closed his talk by stating that the reason his story might be of interest to us is because everyone has a Sahara to cross... perhaps more than one. Everyone eventually goes through their own Sahara, their own private hell, their 'dark night of the soul'.

It is by facing whatever life gives us with courage and determination that we grow more surely towards the stars.

Five years ago, Brian met a wise and wealthy man who had spent his entire life studying success. He reached a clear conclusion concerning the reason for success in life.

He said that the key to success was to set a goal and stay with it until you achieve success at one important thing. Your subconscious mind will then accept that success experience and store it as a pattern of success. From then on, your subconscious will drive and direct you to duplicate the pattern of success in all things you attempt.

Another way of saying it is: *"Nothing succeeds like success."* Psychologists have demonstrated that achievement gives you a natural high. Once you've experienced your first great success, not only are you automatically programmed to repeat it, but nothing else will ever give you the same wonderful feeling of satisfaction.

> "Be careful what you water your dreams with. Water them with worry and fear and you will produce weeds that choke the life from your dream. Water them with optimism and solutions and you will cultivate success. Always be on the lookout for ways to turn a problem into an opportunity for success. Always be on the lookout for ways to nurture your dream."
>
> — Lao Tzu

Each of us has our own idea of what 'success' really means, but I'd like to share with you an inspiring definition of 'success' by 19th century poet, philosopher and essayist, Ralph Waldo Emerson, which I first heard at an MDRT Annual Meeting over 30 years ago.

"To laugh often and much;
To win the respect of intelligent people and the affection of children;

To earn the appreciation of honest critics and endure the betrayal of false friends;
To appreciate beauty;
To find the best in others;
To leave the world a bit better, whether by a healthy child, a garden patch, or a redeemed social condition;
To know even one life has breathed easier because you have lived;
This is to have succeeded."

RALPH WALDO EMERSON

True success is the experience of the miraculous. It is the perception of divinity wherever we go - in the eyes of a child, in the beauty of a flower, in the flight of a bird.

This is beautifully captured by William Wordsworth in his poem, *Daffodils*.

I wandered lonely as a cloud
That floats on high o'er vales and hills,
When all at once I saw a crowd,
A host, of golden daffodils;
Beside the lake, beneath the trees,
Fluttering and dancing in the breeze.

Continuous as the stars that shine
And twinkle on the Milky Way,
They stretched in never-ending line
Along the margin of a bay:
Ten thousand saw I at a glance,
Tossing their heads in sprightly dance.

The waves beside them danced; but they
Out-did the sparkling waves in glee:
A poet could not but be gay,
In such a jocund company:

I gazed - and gazed - but little thought
What wealth the show to me had brought:

For oft, when on my couch I lie
In vacant or in pensive mood,
They flash upon that inward eye
Which is the bliss of solitude;
And then my heart with pleasure fills,
And dances with the daffodils.

— WILLIAM WORDSWORTH

Just the sight of the daffodils is enough to bring forth unbridled joy in the poet, indicating universal love, a feeling of oneness with nature, identifying with all creation.

> "The secret of health for both mind and body is not to mourn for the past, nor to worry about the future, but to live the present moment wisely and earnestly."
>
> — Gautama Buddha

SWAMI RAMA TIRTHA on WORK, SUCCESS and LIFE

As one explores the deeper import of success one will find the thoughts of renowned Indian Sage Swami Rama Tirtha enlightening. He made numerous declarations on success and work.

Swami Rama Tirtha (1873-1906) was a Vedantin of the highest realization, who achieved the pinnacle of human accomplishment, Self-Enlightenment. He is regarded as one of India's greatest sages. Vedanta – the philosophy of life and living, according to him is no dogma or blind faith, but the realization of our true Self, the state of All-Being,

All Knowledge, All Bliss. I quote below some of **Swami Rama Tirtha's profound words of wisdom** – most of these were delivered in talks to enthralled audiences at the **Golden Gate Hall, San Francisco, USA in 1902-1903**.

- "Let your work be impersonal; let your work be free from the taint of selfish egotism; let your work be just like the work of the stars and the sun; let your work be like that of the moon. Then alone can your work be successful."

- "Let the body and mind be continuously at work to such a degree that the labour may not be felt at all."

- "Sacrifice your little self, forget it in the performance of your work, and success must be yours. It cannot be otherwise. The desire for success must die in your work before achieving success."

- "In order that you may have success, in order that you may prosper, you must through your acts, by your own everyday life, burn your own body and muscles, cremate them in the fire of use. You must use them; you must consume your body and mind, put them in a burning state; crucify your body and mind; work, work; and then will light shine through you."

- "O happy worker! success must seek you when you cease to seek success."

- "If you deserve, you need not desire; the objects of desire will be brought to you, will come to you. If you make yourself worthy, help must come to you."

- "The very moment that you rise above the desire, the object of desire seeks you, and the very moment that you assume the craving, seeking, asking, begging attitude, you will be repulsed;

you will not have, you cannot have the object of desire. Rise above the thing, stand above it, and it will seek you. That is the Law."

- "Realise the heaven within you, and all at once all the desires are fulfilled, all the misery and suffering is put an end to."

- "In order that your work should be successful, you should not mind the end, you should not care for the consequences or the result. Let the means and the end be brought together, let the very work be your end."

- "No, the consequence and the result are nothing to me, failure and success are nothing to me; I must work because I love work: I must work for its own sake. To work is my aim, to keep in activity is my life. My Self is energy itself. I must work."

- "Worry not about the consequences, expect nothing from the people, bother not about favourable reviews of your work or severe criticism thereon."

- "Do not, please, make yourselves cringing, sneaking, miserable creatures. As you think, so will you become. Think yourselves to be God and God you are. Think yourselves to be free and free you are this moment. *No one can ever estimate you at a higher value than you set upon yourselves.* Think yourself to be Divinity, have a living faith in your Divinity and nothing can harm you, nobody can injure you."

- Take to your work, not as a plodding labourer but like a noble prince for pleasure's sake, as useful exercise, as a happy play or merry game. Never approach a task in a scared spirit. Be yourself."

- "Forget your little Self in work and entirely throw yourself into it; you will succeed. If you are thinking, become thought itself; you shall succeed. If you are working, become work itself, and thus alone you shall succeed."

"Good thoughts and actions can never produce bad results; bad thoughts and actions can never produce good results ... We understand this law in the natural world, and work with it; but few understand it in the mental and moral world—although its operation there is just as simple and undeviating— and they, therefore, do not cooperate with it."

— **James Allen, As a Man Thinketh**

TEN

OVERCOMING ADVERSITY

"When you go through a hard period, when everything seems to oppose you... when you feel you cannot even bear one more minute, NEVER GIVE UP! Because it is the time and place that the course will divert!"

— 13th-century Persian poet, Jalāl ad-Dīn Rūmī (1207 - 1273)

WMITCHELL, international keynote speaker and author, gave an outstanding presentation at an MDRT Annual Meeting I attended, titled 'It's What You Do About It'. He had everything going for him in 1971 until he was involved in a mototcycle accident and suffered burns over 65% of his body. His face and hands were horribly scarred, his fingers were badly burned and his body was in unbelievable pain. Not only did he survive but went on to achieve great success in life. After his burn accident and recovery, Mitchell completed his training as a pilot and in 1975 co-founded a company called Vermont Castings. The company made energy-efficient wood-burning stoves. He figured out how to use his new and different hands, and was flying an aeroplane. He even bought his own. By 1975, he had made it once again. Believe it or not, another major disaster struck.

He invited four people to fly with him to San Francisco. He was a commercial pilot and a very good one. When the plane was 75 feet in the air, the engine stalled and the plane crashed onto the runway. He managed to get the four passengers off the plane without any injuries, but he couldn't move his legs. He was eventually removed from the plane and told by doctors that he was paralysed from the waist down and would never walk again. Although confined to a wheelchair, he made a remarkable recovery.

Undefeated by the blazing motorcycle accident and paralyzing plane crash, Mitchell learned to take responsibility for the countless changes in his life. Demonstrating his indomitable spirit, remarkable achievements followed his accidents, including the following:

Founding chairman of a $65 million company, a two-term Mayor of a town in Colorado, Congressional Nominee, a radio host and television personality, published author and Speakers Hall of Fame inductee, who has spoken in over 30 countries. He is also a conservation leader and respected environmentalist and served as co-chairman of the National Parks Conservation Association. A popular television personality and radio host, Mitchell makes guest appearances throughout the world. He went on to earn an Executive Masters in Public Administration from the University of Colorado. He is the author of "It's Not What Happens to You, It's What You Do About It."

Mitchell lectures extensively throughout the world on the topic "Taking Responsibility for Change". His message often paraphrases the quote of Epictetus: *"It's not what happens to you, but how you react to it that matters."* In his speaking style, he ensures that the remaining short nubs of his fingers are visible and prominent as he gesticulates and he uses his hands to frequently and vigorously move himself about the stage in his wheelchair. It's an amazing and inspirational sight to behold.

He proves, beyond a doubt, that setbacks can be transformed into exciting new starting points, impossible situations can be overcome and one can successfully move forward. Invited to the White House under five United States Presidents, he continues his love of piloting airplanes and outdoor activities, and served as President of the Global Speakers Federation.

Just before closing his brilliant presentation from the MDRT Main Platform, Mitchell left us with the following words from the German philosopher, Goethe: *"Whatever you can do, or dream you can, begin it. Boldness has genius, power and magic in it."* You see, it's not what happens to you, it's what you do about it that makes the difference.

DEFEAT – KAHLIL GIBRAN

In his poem Defeat, Kahlil Gibran portrays defeat as something that can affect a person positively. Taking an unusual stance towards defeat, the poet's purpose is to change his audience's perspective about what failure actually means. Throughout the poem, Gibran goes through a variety of moods, exemplifying the emotional process that people generally go through when faced with defeat. In each stanza, the poet holds a different point of view towards defeat by adopting a sarcastic tone in the beginning, only to switch it later on to a confident and resilient one; this better portrays the idea that defeat does not have to be tied to negative connotations. Through Gibran's use of personification, paradox, and the ongoing metaphor to the 5 stages of grief, the author is able to convey the idea that he speaks from experience and that defeat can be empowering and something to learn from. (Acknowledgement to Bartleby Research)

DEFEAT

Defeat, my Defeat, my solitude and my aloofness;
You are dearer to me than a thousand triumphs,
And sweeter to my heart than all world-glory.

Defeat, my Defeat, my self-knowledge and my defiance,
Through you I know that I am yet young and swift of foot
And not to be trapped by withering laurels.
And in you I have found aloneness
And the joy of being shunned and scorned.

Defeat, my Defeat, my shining sword and shield,
In your eyes I have read
That to be enthroned is to be enslaved,
And to be understood is to be levelled down,
And to be grasped is but to reach one's fullness
And like a ripe fruit to fall and be consumed.

Defeat, my Defeat, my bold companion,
You shall hear my songs and my cries and my silences,
And none but you shall speak to me of the beating of wings,
And urging of seas,
And of mountains that burn in the night,
And you alone shall climb my steep and rocky soul.

Defeat, my Defeat, my deathless courage,
You and I shall laugh together with the storm,
And together we shall dig graves for all that die in us,
And we shall stand in the sun with a will,
And we shall be dangerous.

KAHLIL GIBRAN

"Happiness does not depend on outward things,
But on the way we see them."

— Leo Tolstoy

Dr Dylan K. Naidoo's Story

The late Dr Dylan Naidoo, Founder and Senior Specialist Dermatologist at Dermatology, Skincare and Laser Specialists (DSC), in Glenwood, Durban, was one of South Africa's foremost medical practitioners.

He came from the humblest beginnings to create one of the most comprehensive, academically and technologically advanced facilities for skin diseases, disorders and skin cancers in the universe, providing a regional, national and international service, with five doctors and 40 staff members.

It was indeed a privilege to have spent many hours over the past 13 years engaging in spirited discussions with Dylan. In the latter years, I was so impressed with his heroic struggle and the incredibly positive manner in which he handled his advanced stage 4 cancer, defying all medical prognoses and actually beating his cancer, that I asked him to contribute this article.

Regarding the amazing practice he created, he said these profound words (refer to Chapters 3 & 4 on Visualization): "I planned mentally and on paper exactly what we have now. Thoughts and visualizations become realities. Try it. It works. Some call this mind power. We are all creators. Use your creative energy. You are the only limitation to growth or your visions. The harder and smarter you work, the luckier you get." You will agree that this is indeed very powerful!

With a passion for the biological sciences, Dr Naidoo pursued a B.Sc. degree in this field, and completed a Masters in Science, funded by bursaries, scholarships and student loans. He then obtained his medical degree at the Nelson R Mandela School of Medicine in Durban and practiced as a general practitioner, developing a passion to thereafter study specialist dermatology for a further four years. He knew that he had found his purpose in life with respect to career - healing patients with the most disabling skin disorders and skin cancers. He says: "Work actually gives me a high or an adrenaline rush. I have never ended up exhausted at the end of the day, even if I am fully booked with no spare time for a cup of tea or lunch."

Dylan was married to Logie Naidoo, Pharmacist at the DSC pharmacy and Practice Manager at DSC and they have one son, Kavi Naidoo, who also excels academically.

> "Our greatest glory is not in never falling, but in rising every time we fall."
>
> — Confucius

Here is Dr Dylan Naidoo's story in his own words, which should serve as inspiration to not only those inflicted with cancer but all readers. It is a clear demonstration of the amazing power we as human beings possess to determine and shape our own destiny.

"I had non-academically qualified, but streetwise parents, who were vendors of fruit, sweets, peanuts and snacks at street corners and school gates; survival was a challenge. I also had to be a street vendor carrying a basket with peanuts and fruit. I had to excel academically at secondary school to gain university entrance."

Regarding his work ethic, he said: "I am self-driven, I propel myself vertically and I want to practice cutting edge medicine, with the latest academic knowledge and technology. In this day and age, you need to update daily or you have lost the edge. This will prevent patients teaching you from 'Google' knowledge. So, for me: satisfaction is death, complacency is a disease and excellence is a moving target. Be in a gel-like state; flow with recent advances and new trends. Change is the only constant in my life. Living is a school of life experience. Be humble, learn from mistakes and errors and be willing to admit that you will do better next time. Crush the ego, believe that we are here to learn and grow, and then you will progress vertically in all respects. I am a 'readerholic'. I have an unrelenting passion to learn almost everything, besides fiction. My library is my precious asset, and it is re-charged with new books and audio CDs on a weekly basis. My favourite shopping site is amazon.com."

He loved quoting Mary Poppins about work attitude:

"In every job that must be done, there must be an element of fun, find the fun and the job's a game, then every task you undertake just becomes a piece of cake."

Cancer Diagnosis

In 2011, aged 53, Dr Naidoo was diagnosed with stage 4 lung cancer and he was given six months to live. Did he succumb to this debilitating and terminal disease or did he fight it with all the power and resources he could marshal? Over 40 months later, he defied the doctor's grim prognosis and was a picture of health. He beat the stage 4 cancer but unfortunately succumbed to pneumonia and passed away peacefully on February 6, 2015.

In his own words, "In 2011, aged 53, I decided to do a normal x-ray as a routine assessment to just check if all was well. I did this test when I was completely well with no symptoms of cancer. After a suspicious x-ray, we conducted scans, biopsies and blood tests. I was then classified as stage 4 cancer, with spread to lymph nodes, with secondaries, or metastases (spread) to all major organs, including multiple brain tumours. I was then informed that my cancer could not be operated on for removal, after a major operation to the chest, together with the removal of a part of a lung. I was then treated with radiation to the chest and the brain, with two courses of chemotherapy, as palliation because there was no cure available. This experience was worse than death, with minimal healing results."

How did he react?

"I immediately accepted the challenge as a part of life, the reality of being human.

I researched every possible treatment idea to heal myself. I began to believe with the end in mind. I declared that I must live beyond the expectations and statistics. I challenged myself to become super-healthy with respect to body, mind and spirit. I conditioned my subconscious mind to expect total healing and recovery. Thoughts become reality, and, as a man thinks, so shall he become. Thoughts and beliefs can change the body. It is possible to use thoughts to change your biology. If you change your biology, you can heal yourself and even stabilise mutant genes that predispose you to getting cancer. These concepts are widely published.

I also took a new drug, a capsule, twice daily. The side effects are 50% of the intravenous chemo experience. This makes it possible for me to work, in a limited capacity. This drug, as well as my positive mental attitude, has reduced my cancer by more than 80%. I am affirmative that a total cure is possible.

The cancer experience was the biggest ever challenge I have faced. My life was in a state of reasonable balance before cancer and I was a reasonable, acceptable human. The cancer made me more humble, more patient, more tolerant, more compassionate and more understanding. It made me respect my body, mind, intellect and spirit even more than before. It taught me more about exercise, health and diet. It taught me to make peace with all on Earth in order to attain peace. It trained me to avoid aggression, confrontation and anger, as these tendencies are the prime destroyers of the human spirit. It also taught me that all things are possible, including healing from stage 4 incurable cancer."

Dylan's words of wisdom above offer lessons for the whole of humanity, as do his following inspiring declarations:

"You get what you radiate. We are all human. We can all experience everything possible on Earth. We are here to learn from the school of life, to become better human beings. Embrace the reality of all our experiences with a problem-solving attitude, to grow and improve the state of your consciousness; then we can fulfil the reason for our existence on this planet. Do not question reality, as it unfolds with any possibility. Do not try to change things that are beyond your control. Change yourself first."

Final profound words from Dr DK Naidoo:

"Inspire others. Create new leaders and not followers. Be happy about the progress of others. The big picture is to create a better planet and universe for us all. We are all connected. Whatever we do affects all of us. Any one person can affect the wellness and happiness of all on Earth. We all need everybody. We must inspire before we expire."

Conclusion:

The true measure of a person, his innermost character and values, can be gauged by how he treats his staff, from the most junior to the most senior. Having had the rare privilege of chatting with many of Dr Dylan's staff, it was astounding to discover the deep reverence and respect everyone, without exception, had for him. Dr Naidoo significantly impacted the lives of every one of them. Each of us has this inherent power to make a huge positive difference in the lives of others.

When Dr. Naidoo sensed that patients were hungry, he gave them his lunch. He often told staff to drop off patients at home if they came by cab. While in consultations with patients, he had an uncanny knack of telling the patient what they were going through emotionally in their personal lives even if he met them for the very first time.

I handed Dr. Dylan a copy of the 1st Edition of Unleash Your Magic soon after it was printed. His response was incredibly positive. Many staff members said he recommended the book to every patient he consulted. He was kind enough to write a book review.

In the final analysis, Dr. Dylan K Naidoo was a truly remarkable human being and an inspiration to all those whose lives he touched. Hopefully, readers will learn some valuable lessons from his amazing life, lessons that will live on in the hearts and minds of all his staff, patients, associates, and readers who are touched by his amazing story.

> "Into the hands of every individual is given a marvellous power for good or evil - the silent, unconscious, unseen influence of his life. This is simply the constant radiation of what man really is, not what he pretends to be."
>
> — William George Jordan

If you experience any major challenges, setbacks or any adversity that may seem insurmountable at the time, reflect on some of the following powerful quotes. You will be amazed at how these positive poems, stories, affirmations and quotes can significantly impact and influence your life for the better - more can be found in Chapters 18 and 19:

I enjoy excellent health. My body is balanced, in total harmony with the Universe. I give thanks for ever increasing health, wealth, beauty and vitality. I am a radiant expression of God. My mind and body now manifest Divine Perfection.

Divine Light and Divine Love flow through me and radiate from me to others and the Universe.

"All power is within you. You can do anything and everything. Believe in that. Do not believe that you are weak. Stand up and express the divinity within you."

— Swami Vivekananda

"All your scholarship would be in vain if at the same time you do not build your character and attain mastery over your thoughts and your actions."

— Mahatma Gandhi

"We are shaped by our thoughts; we become what we think. When the mind is pure, joy follows like a shadow that never leaves."

— Gautama Buddha

"He who conquers others is strong; he who conquers himself is mighty."

— Lao Tzu

"You have to accept whatever comes and the only important thing is that you meet it with courage and with the best that you have to give."

— Eleanor Roosevelt

Also reflect on Norman Cousins' miraculous recovery as outlined in Chapter 14 and the research done on laughter therapy. Ensure you laugh heartily as often as possible.

"I've learnt that no matter what happens or how bad it seems today, life does go on, and it will be better tomorrow. I've learnt that you can tell a lot about a person by the way he/she handles these three things: a rainy day, lost luggage and tangled Christmas tree lights. I've learnt that, regardless of your relationship with your parents, you'll miss them when they're gone from your life. I've learnt that making a 'living' is not the same thing as making a 'life'. I've learnt that life sometimes gives you a second chance. I've learnt that you shouldn't go through life with a catcher's mitt on both hands; you need to be able to throw something back. I've learnt that whenever I decide something with an open heart, I usually make the right decision. I've learnt that even when I have pains, I don't have to be one. I've learnt that every day you should reach out and touch someone. People love a warm hug, or just a friendly pat on the back. I've learnt that I still have a lot to learn. I've learnt that people will forget what you said, people will forget what you did, but people will never forget how you made them feel."

— Maya Angelou

ELEVEN

BUILD A BETTER YOU

"You must live in the present, launch yourself on every wave, find your eternity in each moment. Fools stand on their island of opportunities and look toward another land. There is no other land; there is no other life but this."

— Henry David Thoreau

CHARLIE H FLOWERS was featured as a keynote speaker for first-time attendees. He heard a man say a few years ago: *"If you want to build a better you, then don't step on butterflies."* He used a butterfly to represent self-image, because your image of yourself is as beautiful and fragile as a butterfly. Every human being has one, an image they hold out every waking hour, and it says, in effect: *"This is me; how do you like me?"* We who are adults don't want people to know what we are like inside. To see it really held out, you have to go to little kids. You can see their butterfly rise and fall, dip and soar; they are just as honest as can be.

Have you seen those youngsters? You must have them in your house, the ones who come running home from school - butterfly held high, can't wait to share with whoever is home. But do you know what happens? One day such a kid came running in. He had kicked the winning goal in a soccer game that day, and he had answered all the questions that the teacher had asked. "Mama, Mama!" he called out. His mother was peeling onions for the evening meal. She asked, *"Can't you see that I'm busy?"* It was the greatest day of his life and what she was saying was dreadfully clear: those smelly, tear-provoking onions were more important than this beautiful thing he came running in to share. If you don't believe that hurts, go back to the kid half an hour later and ask, *"What was that you wanted to say, Tom?"* You know what he'll say? *"Oh nothing!"* The bloom is gone. Parent to child, husband to wife, teacher to child! If we really believed in this concept, we wouldn't do the things we do. We generalise and ask, *"Can't you ever do anything right?"* Then we wonder why their butterfly doesn't soar. It's because of what we have done. Instead of continually tramping on people's butterflies, Charlie urges us to uplift them.

We are in the unique position of being with people when their butterflies need lifting, aren't we? Adopting this concept will change one's life. Charlie quoted an article by Woody Woodson entitled *Give and Gain.* He said in every interview you should give as if you were the star actor in a play on Broadway. You should give of your knowledge and your enthusiasm. If you really believe in what you are doing, the prospect is going to know it, so you give and then you gain, not just for the money, but for a life of helping others. We are in a business where we can show others how much we care.

"A particular train of thought persisted in, be it good or bad, cannot fail to produce its results on the character and circumstances. A man cannot directly choose his circumstances, but he can choose his thoughts, and so indirectly, yet surely, shape his circumstances."

— James Allen, <u>As a Man Thinketh</u>

ALAN PRESS, President of the National Association of Life Underwriters (NALU) in the USA, spoke on the title 'commitments'. He stated that, not far from NALU'S national headquarters in Washington DC, is the Arlington National Cemetery. Carved into the wall that forms part of the shimmering reflecting pool at the Robert Kennedy gravesite is the following simple, yet infinitely inspirational message that he thinks is particularly appropriate to every life insurance agent.

It read: "It is from numberless acts of courage and belief that human history is shaped. Each time a man stands for an ideal, or acts to improve the lot of others, or strikes out against injustice, he sends forth a tiny ripple of hope, and crossing each other from a million different centres of energy and daring, those ripples build a current that can sweep down the mightiest walls of oppression and resistance."

When an agent goes out to sell insurance, it is an act of courage. It is an act of belief. Each time we sell a life or a health insurance policy, we make a difference in the lives of others. Each life agent is the centre of energy, and every life agent is a centre of daring.

We build walls; walls of hope, walls of financial security. We send kids to school and college. We pay medical bills. We keep families together. We make it possible for clients to retire with self-respect and grace. Yes, we even make it possible for them to die with dignity.

While we are on the subject of courage, there was this story of the billionaire who owned a 1, 500-acre ranch in Tucson. One day, he was showing some guests around. He showed them an enormous swimming pool he had on the grounds, but, in this pool, there were huge alligators.

The man explained: "The one thing I value the most is courage, guts. It's the one thing that pushed me to the top. Just to prove how much I value guts and courage, if anyone swims across this pool and makes it out on the other side alive, I will buy him anything he wants."

Of course, nobody moved. As the man and his guests turned to return to the house, they heard a splash. Everyone looked around and saw one of the guests swimming desperately across the pool, dodging the alligators. After a few death-defying minutes, the swimmer reached the other end of the pool and got out.

"You did it!" the host said. "You're the most courageous man I've met! Just tell me what you want and it's yours."

"The only thing I want," the man said, "is to know who the hell pushed me into that pool!"

Sometimes in life, we have to take risks. Analyse your options and don't have somebody else 'push' you. Be the master of your own destiny.

"You are a volume in the divine book
A mirror to the power that created the universe
Whatever you want, ask it of yourself
Whatever you're looking for can only be found
Inside of you."

— Rumi

The following poem demonstrates what the ideal state of one's mind should be and is one of the true masterpieces of the Elizabethan era. It speaks to many aspects of life: conscience, contentment, determining when 'enough is enough', giving, understanding one's priorities in life, the powers of imagination and so much more. It can also help us overcome adversities, and perhaps even shield us from experiencing unnecessary stress and strain.

MY MIND TO ME A KINGDOM IS SIR EDWARD DYER (D. 1607)

My mind to me a kingdom is;
Such present joys therein I find,
That it excels all other bliss
That earth affords or grows by kind:
Though much I want that most would have,
Yet still my mind forbids to crave.

No princely pomp, no wealthy store,
No force to win the victory,
No wily wit to salve a sore,
No shape to feed a loving eye;
To none of these I yield as thrall;
For why? My mind doth serve for all.

I see how plenty surfeits oft,
And hasty climbers soon do fall;
I see that those which are aloft
Mishap doth threaten most of all:
They get with toil, they keep with fear:
Such cares my mind could never bear.

Content I live, this is my stay;
I seek no more than may suffice;

I press to bear no haughty sway;
Look, what I lack my mind supplies.
Lo, thus I triumph like a king,
Content with that my mind doth bring.

Some have too much, yet still do crave;
I little have, and seek no more.
They are but poor, though much they have,
And I am rich with little store;
They poor, I rich; they beg, I give;
They lack, I leave; they pine, I live.

I laugh not at another's loss,
I grudge not at another's gain;
No worldly waves my mind can toss;
My state at one doth still remain:
I fear no foe, I fawn no friend;
I loathe not life, nor dread my end.

Some weigh their pleasure by their lust,
Their wisdom by their rage of will;
Their treasure is their only trust,
A cloaked craft their store of skill;
But all the pleasure that I find
Is to maintain a quiet mind.

My wealth is health and perfect ease,
My conscience clear, my chief defence;
I neither seek by bribes to please,
Nor by deceit to breed offence:
Thus do I live; thus will I die;
Would all did so as well as I!

SIR EDWARD DYER (D. 1607)

Robert Smith emphasises the importance of understanding and facing our own mortality in this beautiful poem:

The Clock of Life

"The clock of life is wound but once,
And no man has the power
To tell just when the hands will stop
At late or early hour.

To lose one's wealth is sad indeed,
To lose one's health is more,
To lose one's soul is such a loss
That no man can restore.

The present only is our own,
So live, love, toil with a will,
Place no faith in "Tomorrow,"
For the Clock may then be still."

ROBERT H. SMITH

TWELVE

2001 MDRT ANNUAL MEETING

A Native American elder once described his own inner struggles in this manner: 'Inside of me, there are two dogs. One of the dogs is mean and evil. The other dog is good. The mean dog fights the good dog all the time.' When asked which dog wins, he reflected for a moment and replied, 'The one I feed the most.'"

— George Bernard Shaw

The 2001 MDRT Annual Meeting in Anaheim, California ranks as one of my favourite meetings. What an experience! It is amazing how MDRT is able to pull out all the stops to deliver a programme of such inspiration, magnitude and splendour.

The attendance of 7, 194 delegates amounted to the largest ever at an Annual Meeting up to that time. Of these, 2, 500 were first-time attendees - another record. Also, for the first time in MDRT history, non-American delegates were in the majority. Of course, since then, MDRT has become a truly global organisation.

A brief summary of some of the main platform presentations follows:

TONY GORDON, presiding MDRT President and an industry legend, shared with delegates how it took him eight years to get to MDRT - he had experienced a mediocre first few years. His 'Secrets of Success': BGO = Blinding Glimpse of the Obvious. He received this profound piece of advice from an Italian friend, Antonio, who restores buildings in Italy: *"I never worry about business. I only worry about doing the job well. If I do the job well, I'll never have to worry about business."*

Tony stated that our expertise and great strengths lie in the management of relationships of trust. The more newspapers write about our business, the more business we write. We have the unique ability to create and maintain relationships. Clients don't buy because they understand... they buy because they are understood. Find people who have money now, or will have money in the future. The way we value ourselves is by how much business we will write. Our success begins with the value that we place on what we do. No one will place a higher value on us than we ourselves. The most important thing in life is not what we achieve in business, but the love we give to our family and fellow man.

Sales idea: The sales process is left brain thinking; decision-making is right brain. How do you move a client from left to right? Tony makes out a cheque to the IRS for $1 million and slides it across the table: *"Mr and Mrs Prospect, this is the cheque your children will have to write to the IRS when you are gone."* Then he reaches out and takes the cheque out of their hands. *"I'll make sure your children will NOT have to write out that cheque."* Life insurance is the greatest vehicle on the planet to pass assets from one generation to another.

Recommended approach to friends and close associates:

"I have no reason to expect you to do business with me because we are friends/belong to the same charitable organisation/etc. But, I didn't think you would respect me if I didn't ask. Because of the nature of the business I'm in, I'd rather call on you three years too early than one day too late. Would you have any objection to getting together with me on a professional basis?"

There are prospects all around - make no assumptions.

> "Don't waste your life in doubts and fears: spend yourself on the work before you, well assured that the right performance of this hour's duties will be the best preparation for the hours or ages that follow it."
>
> — **Ralph Waldo Emerson**

ANDY LORD, incoming Top of the Table (TOT) Chair, posed the Million Dollar Conference question: *"How do you get in front of new people?"* The difference between Top of the Table (TOT – 6 x base MDRT production)) and MDRT = the number of new qualified prospects seen each week. How do we get new people in the door? He shared eight basic prospecting strategies, some of which include: cold calling, direct mail, referrals and seminars. He was writing up business for 350 - 400 lives a year - hard work - exhausting. He then realised certain facts that were clearly obvious:

- Rich people have more money than poor people.

- Older people have more money than young people.

- Rich insurance agents have more money than poor insurance agents.

- TOT members have six times more appointments than MDRT members.

Andy only does seminars. His advice was that we pick a strategy that works for us, work hard, and we will benefit.

FRANK MILES, a professional variety comedian with numerous TV and Las Vegas credits, gave a great presentation. He used to be very afraid of people; he wouldn't even ask the time. True courage, he came to realise, is not in facing death; true courage lies in facing life. He came onto the stage juggling knives - he said one has to focus on the handles, not the blades. Every fear has a handle.

Frank was in a serious hang-gliding accident. He was more afraid of living than dying. Hang-gliding without training? What the heck, he thought. He flew and crashed just two hours away from a hospital. He died in the emergency room, but was somehow revived by the doctors. He says the reason he was brought back to life was - he was uninsured. He doesn't know why he was given that second chance.

Frank got Brian Ashe (Past MDRT President) to lie flat on his back on the stage. He took Brian's watch. He then juggled the bowling ball, the watch and the ping pong ball. He dropped the ball deliberately close to Brian. He continued juggling. He said that we need to look at things with the proper perspective. Brian did not worry about his watch. He got perspective.

We don't make mistakes... we spend mistakes... by learning.

There is no best choice. We can't know how everything will work out in the end - that is up to a higher power.

"There is something in the human spirit that will survive and prevail, there is a tiny and brilliant light burning in the heart of man that will not go out no matter how dark the world becomes."

— Leo Tolstoy

KIM PHUC: On 8 June 1972, a photograph of a nine-year-old fleeing a napalm strike in South Vietnam startled the editors of newspapers around the world. It was featured prominently on all the front pages, accompanied by a dramatic and unfolding historic story. That girl was Kim Phuc, who recounted her incredible story from the main platform.

Her house was destroyed by a napalm bomb. Temperatures reached 800°C. She was taken to hospital and left to die. Fortunately, her father got help and took her to the Burn Clinic in Hanoi (then Saigon). She was in excruciating pain all the time, often passing out, and remained in hospital for 14 months, undergoing seventeen operations for fourth degree burns on half of her body. She recounted that her biggest fear was that she'd never be loved or be able to have a baby. She really wanted to become a doctor, but the authorities cut short her studies. She was monitored 24 hours a day and reached a low point in her life. Kim married in 1992. She later defected to Toronto, Canada, with her two sons and her mum and dad - all of whom were at the MDRT Annual Meeting.

She stated that forgiveness is an important step towards peace and quoted Luke 6:27–28: *"Love your enemies."* She found it impossible to forgive - too much pain and scarring, and asked of herself, *"How can I love?"* She asked God to help her forgive and, finally, she did. Prior to that, she was filled with hatred and anger - she said God's love solved that. She stated that, while napalm is very powerful, faith and forgiveness are much more so. At the 1996 memorial, she met the pilot who co-ordinated the bombings that nearly killed her and personally forgave him - we were shown a video of the touching encounter.

"My life should show you that forgiveness is more powerful than any weapon of war."

She forgave all the people who caused her suffering. She said forgiveness will heal all those close to you, most importantly, yourself. She founded the Kim Foundation to help child victims of war around world.

RONAN TYNAN, of Ireland, had both legs amputated. His story is an example of dogged perseverance in the face of insurmountable obstacles.

He came onto the main platform singing in spectacular fashion. He credits his success to the belief others had in him. He enjoyed the love of family and friends. His father kept encouraging him by repeating, *"You're great."* You will see in yourself what others see in you - an inner strength waiting to be harnessed. He looked at what he had instead of what he wanted. He cautioned that, if we focus too much on what we want, we will feel very dissatisfied most of the time. He advised us to focus on building our physical, mental and spiritual strengths.

He dared to dream of riding in the Grand National, but did not have a horse large enough to carry his weight.

He shared some important lessons:

- Don't be slow in using and accepting encouragement - you have no idea of the benefits.

- Focus on endless possibilities; he now revels in the fact that his physical challenges made him take risks.

- If we focus more on what we have in life, we will get so much more.

- Life is driven from the inside.

- If you focus on being happy, it seeps out and people gravitate towards you.... You will find inner peace.

- Concentrate on the task at hand - give it your best... 100%.

Ronan learnt to dance while training for discus. He had not only the will to win, but the will to prepare to win. He said it's not just enough to prepare... we must believe in our goal with heart and soul.

Between 1981 and 1984, Ronan amassed 18 gold medals and 14 world records in international track and field events. While studying at the National College of Physical Education as a medical student, he began to take voice lessons - his natural talent shone through. In 1996, Ronan was invited to be part of the famous Pavarotti School. His rapid rise to prominence led to Sony Music offering him a recording deal.

"Once you make a decision, the universe conspires to make it happen."

— Ralph Waldo Emerson

BRUCE ETHERINGTON, another MDRT legend, spoke on the topic 'from acorns to oak trees'. Bruce was a Charter member of Top of the Table and qualified every single year of its existence. He states that the most important question you can ever ask clients is the three-year question:

"Mr Client, if we were sitting here three years from today, what would have happened over the previous three years in your business and personal life for you to believe you had achieved good or excellent progress?"

Bruce gets a 100% positive response with a 98% closure rate. Response times range from one to 59 minutes. This question allows clients to find their passion.

Bruce drew an analogy with golf to make a powerful point. The average golfer, over 18 holes, uses the driver 14% of the time and the putter 35% to 50% of the time. However, most training time is spent on the driving range, NOT the putting green. This is wrong. The question is: *"Where are you allocating most of your time in this business?"*

Bruce closed his powerful presentation with an acronym: SWEAT.

Sight - What is your sight focussed on? Focus on four areas of life.

Work - Put great effort into what you do.

Enthusiasm - Comes from the Greek *En Theos* - 'The God Within'.

Attitude - Attitude, NOT aptitude, determines your altitude.

Tenacity - Never, never, never... give up.

The next speaker, **JIM ROGERS**, qualified for Top of the Table for 20 consecutive years. He was very involved in industry associations, spending only two days each week in the office, and the remaining three days contributing to industry.

His lessons to delegates:

- Ensure that your business activity has purpose and meaning.

- Develop a daily work routine - continually refine it until it becomes second nature.

- Always use a meeting agenda.

- Delegate - do what you do best, delegate the rest; what will market pay to have that done?

- Specialise - business is becoming more and more complex. Determine which part of the business you have a passion for and get the assistance you need. Leading producers specialise in niche markets.

- Maintain a consistent professional image.

- Be a professional advisor; be on the same side as the client in solving his or her problem.

- Build trust.

- Be transparent - engage in complete disclosure and include alternative recommendations.

- Always say 'thank you'.

TONY CHRISTIANSEN was run over by a train at the age of nine, losing both his legs. He was rushed to hospital. He wanted to scratch his foot - there was nothing there. He came onto the stage in a wheelchair, then proceeded to climb up some scaffolding and sat on a piece of plank.

He learnt to swim. After five months, he swam a mile. He then thought of participating in the Olympics and was introduced to the disabled sports movement. This became a reality when he was part of the 1980 Paralympics in the finals of the 100m breaststroke. He said it's all about attitude. Many people are far worse off than he is.

He wanted to work and he applied to a sign writing company, who initially did not want to hire him due to his handicap. Eventually, he got in, then bought the company and owned it for 10 years. He sold it in 1999 for millions of dollars. He says we judge people - we put them in boxes and label them 'handicapped'.

His advice:

- Share our passions and beliefs.

- Believe success will come to everyone.

- Learn from our experiences - one never fails.

- Be the best we can be.

- It's not what happens to us, it's what we do about it that's important.

- Life's not easy, nor is it fair.

- Don't give up on your dreams, and don't let other people take them away.

- It's not what you drive, it's what drives you!

Tony is currently one of Australia's leading motivational speakers. He is a successful businessman, best-selling author, qualified lifeguard, Olympic Gold Medallist in shot put, discus and javelin, and a second-degree black belt in Tae Kwon Do. He is in constant demand as a keynote speaker. Tony leaves his audiences with insight of what can be achieved with determination, belief, and a burning desire to accept and succeed at the challenges of life.

MICHAEL GELB stated that Leonardo da Vinci was history's greatest genius. He shared seven principles for thinking like Leonardo da Vinci:

1. Curiosita - curiosity.

2. Dimonstrazione - demonstration - question everything; become an original thinker.

3. Sensasione - sensation; cross reference senses; be sharp.

4. Sfumato - fumes, like 'going up in smoke'; mysterious quality.

5. Arte/Scienza - art/science; study the science of art, and the art of science; use left and right brain.

6. Corporalita - balance body and mind; learn to preserve your own health; avoid grievous bodily harm and keep your mind cheerful; exercise moderately.

7. Connessione - connection; as you search for truth and beauty, realise that everything connects with everything else.

Businesses usually spend weeks setting up a vision/mission statement. The real question is: how much time do YOU spend on your vision/mission and strategy for living them with passion? Remember, the most important connection is with a Higher Power. Spend lots of time writing down your vision/mission. This will be the greatest investment you can make in your life.

"Where the mind is without fear and the head is held high;
Where knowledge is free;
Where the world has not been broken up into fragments
By narrow domestic walls;
Where words come out from the depth of truth;
Where tireless striving stretches its arms towards perfection;
Where the clear stream of reason has not lost its way
Into the dreary desert sand of dead habit;

Where the mind is led forward by thee
Into ever-widening thought and action—
Into that heaven of freedom, my Father, let my country awake."

— Nobel Prize Winner Rabindranath Tagore, Gitanjali

IAN PERCY, rated one of the Top 21 speakers of the 21st century, speaks to and consults with corporations around the world, helping them to new levels of purpose and passion. A Registered Psychologist with degrees in education and theology, Ian is one of the world's pioneers in integrating spirituality into business and everyday life and the author of many bestsellers, including *The Seven Secrets to a Life of Meaning*.

He states that 90 to 95% of people live, work and die not knowing why they were put on this Earth. Life should be full of joy, purpose and meaning, and should involve the leaving of a legacy. Quest for meaning is the driving force, the inner purpose. How do we find this meaning? He listed six things - stages of our inner journey - that will help us achieve real purpose and meaning in our lives:

INNOCENCE: As a kid, everybody loves me. Mum feeds me today and tomorrow. In my childlike eyes, my parents are God. How long does this innocence last? Until the first break at school, when some child teases or beats me up. Response: *"Learn to look out for myself."* This is when innocence begins to die.

INDEPENDENCE: We separate ourselves from others and learn not to trust all people. We find ways to distinguish ourselves from everyone else. Then we go on to find ourselves.

INSTITUTION: There are four major ones: family, school, work and religion. People within these institutions can reward or punish our behaviour. We experience tough times and other people's ideas and expectations are forced upon us: *'you will do maths'* - *'but I like music'* - *'sit down and do maths'*. We must fit in and not rock the boat. Tension begins brewing.

IRRITATION: We're restless. We don't know what's wrong. *"I don't fit; I'm angry, irritated; I'm not doing the right thing; I am a successful businessman worth millions - but now what? Why am I doing this?"*

Restlessness is a divine source of energy; it is destiny calling you. What angers or frustrates you about the world? Don't run away from your feelings; run towards them. Nothing happens if you don't get angry. We have lights because Edison was fed up with working in the dark. What are you angry about? I'm angry that 90 to 95% will never know why we are here. What angers you? Is it a family left without means because you did not insure the breadwinner? A business collapse? Someone who is disabled - with no income? Change the world!

INSIGHT: We can reject what our parents taught us. What do you want to do differently? What do you suggest? Irritation should always lead to insight.

INTEGRATION: This is the feeling that life just makes sense - a sense of alignment, a connection to all things.

Everyone is somewhere in this sequence. Where are you now? To find real meaning in your life, look at what makes you restless. It virtually always has nothing to do with success or income level; there is a higher purpose to your life. Always remember: "You are never empty; you are never alone."

Ian closed his presentation with a quote from Gary Zukov's internationally acclaimed book, *The Seat of the Soul*:

> "When the deepest part of you becomes engaged in what you are doing, when your activities and actions become gratifying and purposeful, when what you do serves both yourself and others, when you do not tire within, but seek the sweet satisfaction of your life and your work, you are doing what you were meant to be doing. The personality that is engaged in the work of the soul is buoyant. It is not burdened with negativity. It does not fear. It experiences purposefulness and meaning. It delights in its work and in others. It is fulfilled and fulfilling."

— **Gary Zukov *"The Seat of the Soul"***

I'd like to add another quote from the same book, the concluding paragraphs:

> "Allow yourself to become aware of what you feel. Give yourself permission to choose the most positive behaviour in each moment. As you discharge negative energy consciously and set your intentions according to what your heart tells you, as you challenge and release your fears and choose to heal, you align your personality with your soul and move towards becoming a being of the light, fully whole and empowered and inwardly secure. Humbleness, forgiveness, clarity and love, all the gifts of the spirit, take root and bloom, and you draw to yourself the universe's greatest gift: human beings with open hearts.

> "Rather than a soul in a body, become a body in a soul. Reach for your soul. Reach even farther. The impulse of creation and power authentic - the hourglass point between energy and matter: that is the seat of the soul. What does it mean to touch that place?

> "It is exciting to come of age spiritually."

— **Gary Zukov *"The Seat of the Soul"***

THIRTEEN

THINK BIG

"There is no end to education. It is not that you read a book, pass an examination, and finish with education. The whole of life, from the moment you are born to the moment you die, is a process of learning."

— **Jiddu Krishnamurti**

Benjamin Carson shared his remarkable and inspiring story at the 1994 MDRT Annual Meeting in Dallas, Texas. Benjamin, an African-American boy, was born in Detroit, Michigan, where he grew up. His mother, Sonya, had dropped out of school in the third grade, and married when she was only 13. When Benjamin Carson was just eight, his parents divorced, and Mrs Carson was left to raise Benjamin and his older brother, Curtis, on her own. She worked at two, sometimes three, jobs at a time as a domestic worker to provide for her boys and to avoid going on the dole.

His family then moved to Boston to live with relatives. His mum always encouraged Ben and his brother to study and further themselves. However, they were very naughty boys - they watched countless TV programmes, played games, and Ben loved playing with rocks - they lived by a railway line. To top it all, Ben did no homework. The net result, as could be expected, was that Ben Carson had no competition for last position in his 5th Grade class. If Ben Carson was in your class, you were guaranteed not to come last. His classmates called him 'dummy'. He developed a violent, uncontrollable temper.

When Mrs Carson was made aware of Benjamin's failing grades, she was determined to turn her sons' lives around. She prayed for some divine inspiration and set new rules for the boys:

1. They could watch only two TV programmes a week.

2. They must visit the local library, borrow and read two books a week and give her a written report at the end of the week.

Even though they were naughty, the boys never thought of disobeying her. Ben, though, was very ingenious. He came up with a way that would fool his mum. He visited the library and borrowed books with pictures only and duly made a report at the end of week. His mom *pretended* to read the report, as she was illiterate, and continually encouraged him. It so happened that Ben got books only on nature, rocks and so on. Very soon, he borrowed books that had more writing and he read the legends underneath the pictures. In no time, he was devouring books on rocks from the library. He read everything in the library about rocks and nature. Unfortunately, 'rocks' was not a subject in school, so his grades were not improving; he was still coming last in class.

A turning point, and a defining moment in his life, occurred when the science teacher came to class with a rock. "Can anyone identify this rock?" she asked. The A, B, C and D students had no answer. Ben was amazed. He knew something they didn't. He raised his hand. The whole class turned around to look at this phenomenon. It had never happened before, let alone to a question they did not know the answer to. Eventually, the teacher turned to him. "Yes, Carson, what's the answer?"

"*Obsidian*," he said. There was total silence. It sounded good, but no one knew if it was correct. The teacher confirmed that it was. "*Can anyone tell me how this rock is formed?*" the teacher then asked. Naturally, the A, B, C and D students did not know, as they couldn't even identify the rock. Carson had his hand up. Eventually, the teacher got to him. He explained, "*It is formed through volcanic eruptions. As the hot lava hits the water, it solidifies and forms obsidian.*" He was an expert on rocks and he went on for many minutes explaining how the rock forms.

"*It was at that moment that I realized I wasn't stupid,*" he recalled later. He asked himself a simple question: "*If I can learn so much about rocks by reading about them, what if I read about my maths, geography, science, history and other subjects?*" He continued to amaze his classmates with his newfound knowledge and, within 18 months, by the end of Grade 6, Benjamin Carson had no competition for first place in his class.

The hunger for knowledge had taken hold of him, and he began to read voraciously on all subjects. He was determined to become a physician, and he learnt to control the violent temper that still threatened his future. After graduating with honours from his high school, he attended Yale University, where he earned a degree in psychology.

From Yale, he went to the Medical School of the University of Michigan, where his interest shifted from psychiatry to neurosurgery. His excellent hand-eye co-ordination and three-dimensional reasoning skills made him a superior surgeon and he went on to achieve great distinction in his life. At age 32, he was appointed as the youngest ever Director of Paediatric Neurosurgery at Johns Hopkins Hospital in Baltimore - one of the foremost institutions in the world in brain research.

He is regarded as one of the world's great surgeons. It was such a great pleasure to meet him and having a picture taken with him after his speech. What a remarkable human being. Had it not been for his mother's perseverance, he would have been a statistic... a nothing... possibly a drug addict, or whatever. The question arises: how many Benjamin Carson's do we have in our midst?

Logan Meeting Dr Ben Carson after his brilliant presentation at the 1994 MDRT Annual Meeting in Dallas, Texas

In 1987, Carson made medical history with an operation to separate a pair of Siamese twins. The Binder twins were born joined at the back of the head. Operations to separate twins joined in this way had always failed, resulting in the death of one or both of the infants. Carson agreed to undertake the operation. A 70-member surgical team, led by Dr Carson, worked for 22 hours. At the end, the twins were successfully separated and now survive independently.

Carson's other surgical innovations have included the first intra-uterine procedure to relieve pressure on the brain of a hydrocephalic foetal twin, and a hemispherectomy, in which an infant suffering from uncontrollable seizures has half of its brain removed. This stops the seizures, and the remaining half of the brain actually compensates for the missing hemisphere.

In addition to his medical practice, Dr Carson is in constant demand as a public speaker, and devotes much of his time to meeting with groups of young people. He has received numerous honours and many awards over the years, including over 61 honorary doctorate degrees. In 2008, the White House announced that Benjamin Carson would receive the Presidential Medal of Freedom, the nation's highest civilian honour, which was conferred on him by President George Bush.

Dr Carson's books include a memoir, *Gifted Hands*, on which the 2009 movie *"Gifted Hands: The Ben Carson Story,"* starring Cuba Gooding Jr. in the lead role, is based. He received the Presidential Medal of Freedom in 2008.

"The outer conditions of a person's life will always be found to be harmoniously related to his inner state...Men do not attract that which they want, but that which they are."

— James Allen

Dr Carson attributed his success to what he condensed into an acronym: THINK BIG!

T is for **Talent**: Our Creator has endowed all of us not just with the ability to sing, dance or throw a ball, but with intellectual talent. Learn to recognise and accept your God-given talents. Develop them and use them. Start getting in touch with that part of you that is intellectual and develop it.

H is for **Honesty**: Lead a clean and honest life; don't have skeletons in the closet. If you have skeletons in the closet, they will definitely come back, just when you don't want to see them, and ruin your life.

I is for **Insight**: It comes from people who have already gone where you're trying to go; learn from their triumphs and their mistakes.

N is for **Nice**: Be nice to all people. If you're nice to people, then, once they get over the suspicion of why you're being nice, they will be nice to you. Remember, people don't care how much you know until they know how much you care. It's nice to be important, but more important to be nice. Be nice to little people; you're still one of them.

K is for **Knowledge**: Knowledge is the key to understanding. It is the key to all your dreams, hopes and aspirations. It makes you a more valuable person. The more knowledge you have, the more people need you. It's an interesting phenomenon, but, when people need you, they pay you, so you'll be okay in life.

B is for **Books**: The learning derived from books is generally much more substantial than from any other source. Books hold the collective knowledge of our world.

I is for **In-depth Learning**: Learn for the sake of knowledge and understanding, rather than for the sake of impressing people or taking a test. This occurs when one actually wants to understand concepts and principals and wants to acquire greater knowledge.

G is for **God**: It is important to realise that God is a real entity, capable of doing anything. Never get too big for God. Don't let ego get in the way. EGO stands for 'edging God out'. Never drop him out of your life. God works miracles for all of us.

Benjamin Carson has served as United States Secretary of Housing and Urban Development from March 2017 to January 2021. He was a candidate for President of the United States in the 2016 Republican primaries. He is considered a pioneer in the field of neurosurgery.

> "Education is the most powerful weapon that you can use to change the world."
>
> — **Nelson Mandela**

FOURTEEN

LAUGHTER AND HUMOUR

"The human race has only one really effective weapon, and that is laughter. The moment it arises, all our hardnesses yield, all our irritations and resentments slip away, and a sunny spirit takes their place."

— Mark Twain

It's not what happens to us, but our response to what happens that determines how we handle life. Our interpretation is crucial. For example, if we ride on a roller coaster, and at the deepest core of our being we feel joy and exhilaration, our bodies start manufacturing dopamine, endorphins and other powerful chemicals that stimulate the immune system. If, on the other hand, we feel terror, our bodies manufacture cortisol and adrenaline, which deplete and can ultimately destroy the immune system. When confronted by something, choose your response very carefully. We human beings are the only species that has the incredible capacity to think, to make choices - choices that could make the difference between sickness and health, life and death.

Let's talk a little about laughing. Most of us are perhaps much too sane, much too serious. Please do not take this life too seriously

- none of us is going to come out of it alive. We need to lighten up a bit. Enjoy life. Scientific studies have shown that the positive beneficial effects of laughter are immeasurable. Every time you laugh, you are thinking better, more creatively. Humour takes the stress out of you and makes you healthier. It produces endorphins that stimulate the immune system. Laughing, alone, can increase the T-cells - the rulers of the immune system - by up to 300%. However, the healthy chemical changes take place only when you laugh out loud.

> "Keep your face always toward the sunshine – and shadows will fall behind you."
>
> — Walt Whitman

Norman Cousins enlightened the medical community about the healing potential of laughter in his book, *Anatomy of an Illness*. In it, he presents a fascinating story of how he laughed his way to health out of a progressive, crippling disease, which the doctors declared as incurable. Cousins, an American journalist, went to the USSR (Russia) in 1964 on an official visit. He developed a fever and was compelled to return to the US. His condition grew from bad to worse. He was hospitalised, but his condition continued to worsen until he felt, as he said, as though a truck had run over every one of his limbs. His entire body pained and his fever kept mounting. The doctors diagnosed the disease as collagen, a systematic degenerative disease of the body's connecting tissue.

The doctors advised him that recovery from this disease required a miracle, and that there was barely one chance in 500 that he would live through this disease. Pain-killing drugs and other medications were administered, but there was no improvement in his condition. His doctors finally advised him they had no cure for his condition. He refused to accept his grim prognosis, and decided to take charge of his own treatment, working in partnership with his physician. After reading Hans Selye's 1956 book, *The Stress of Life*, about the body's response to stress, Cousins recalled that research had shown that negative emotions could create chemical changes, which would eventually lead to adrenal exhaustion.

He began to reason with himself that, if tension, anxiety and worry pull a man down and make him sick, the converse should also be true. **Laughter, cheerfulness, joy, love, confidence, festivity, faith, hope, courage, tenacity and a strong will to live should pull a man up and cure him of the most incurable of diseases.** He kept himself cheerful. With this in mind, Cousins watched films of the Marx Brothers and *Candid Camera*. He had nurses read to him from humorous books. He played practical jokes and told jokes. Lo and behold, he began feeling better. After each laughing episode, he noted that he could sleep comfortably without the need for analgesia or sedation. Blood tests showed that his sedimentation rate (an index of the degree of infection or inflammation in the body) decreased after his laughter. Within a few weeks, he reduced his medicinal dosage significantly, and, within a few months, he was back at work.

> "Laughter is a form of internal jogging. It moves your internal organs around. It enhances respiration. It is an igniter of great expectations."
>
> — **Norman Cousins**

After his recovery, Cousins spent 12 years of his life at UCLA Medical School in the Department of Behavioural Medicine, exploring the scientific proof of his belief. He established the Humour Research Task Force, which co-ordinated and supported worldwide clinical research on humour.

Cousins, although one of the best-known proponents of using positive emotions to improve health, was certainly not the first to assert such a relationship. As early as the 1300's, Henri de Mondeville, royal surgeon to French kings and professor of anatomy and surgery at the University of Montpellier, wrote: "Let the surgeon take care to regulate the whole regimen of the patient's life for joy and happiness, allowing his relatives and special friends to cheer him, and by having someone tell him jokes."

> "The tragedy of life is not death - but what we let die inside of us while we live."
>
> — Norman Cousins

William McDougall, professor of psychology at Harvard, wrote in 1922: "The possession of this peculiar disposition shields us from the depressing influence which the many minor mishaps and shortcomings of our fellows would exert upon us if we did not possess it.... It not only prevents our minds from dwelling upon these depressing objects, but it actually converts these objects into stimulants that promote our well-being, both bodily and mentally, instead of depressing us through sympathetic pain or distress. Laughter is primarily and fundamentally the antidote of sympathetic pain."

> "If you wish to glimpse inside a human soul and get to know the man, don't bother analyzing his ways of being silent, of talking, of weeping, or seeing how much he is moved by noble ideas; you'll get

better results if you just watch him laugh. If he laughs well, he's a good man...All I claim to know is that laughter is the most reliable gauge of human nature."

— **Fyodor Dostoevsky (1821-1881 - Russian novelist, short story writer, essayist, and journalist)**

Today, many decades after Cousins' experience, we have the scientific research to explain the specific physiological changes that his anecdotal story suggested. Laughter does affect the body, mind and spirit.

Dr Lee S Berk and fellow researcher, Dr Stanley Tan of Loma Linda University in California, have been studying the effects of laughter on the immune system. I have followed their research for over 25 years. To date, their published studies have shown that laughing lowers blood pressure, reduces stress hormones, increases muscle flexion and boosts immune function by raising levels of infection-fighting T-cells, disease-fighting proteins called gamma-interferon, and B-cells, which produce disease-destroying antibodies. Laughter also triggers the release of endorphins, the body's natural painkillers, and produces a general sense of well-being.

Below is an article titled **Laughter: A fool-proof prescription** by Janelle Ringer, published in Loma Linda University Health on April 1, 2019, in which Dr. Berk is interviewed on his research into the benefits of laughter.

We all know the saying "laughter is the best medicine," but have you ever wondered how many body systems it really benefits? Laughter has a huge impact on both mental and physical health, and is possibly the cheapest medicine available, aside from fresh air, sunshine or exercise.

Lee S. Berk, DrPH, associate dean of research affairs for Loma Linda University School of Allied Health Professions, is serious about laughter. Berk has been studying the effect laughter has on the body since 1988, appearing in media outlets from TIME and USA Today to Forbes and NBC. He encourages people to laugh every day. Laughter can make you feel good in the present, build up good health in the future, and work to combat negative health from the past.

Berk sits in an office cluttered with a collection of signs and gimmicks, including RX prescription bottles for laughter, corked jars of laughter, and joke books from the past several decades. Berk sat down to start off National Humour Month by answering some of the most common questions he gets about his laughter research. Here are some edited excerpts from an interview:

What made you decide to research laughter?

Lee Berk: When I started my career in healthcare, I used to emphasize the importance of the physical factors of health. As my career and knowledge matured, I spent more time learning how factors like lifestyle, diet, gratitude, spirituality, attitude, and forgiveness could also play roles in health and disease outcomes. My idea to study laughter was also inspired by the Bible. In Proverbs 17:22, the author writes, "A merry heart does good, like medicine, but a broken spirit dries the bones." This refers to the integrative medical science of psycho-neuro-immunology being stated in biblical terms. This was the starting point and is the core of whole person care of mind, body and spirit. Just like people with depression have a greater propensity to have a compromised immune system, my research came to show that people who experience joyful laughter have biological translations and can impact positive responses of the immune system.

Who was the first researcher to look at laughter as a medicine?

The subject was first introduced when a man named Norman Cousins was diagnosed with an autoimmune disease in the 1960s. He was the editor of *The Saturday Review* and he had a life of massive stress and distress, so he hypothesized that he would need to produce good stress — eustress — to see if he could reverse this prognosis.

I first met him in 1989 when he came here to ask me if there were any known physiological benefits from laughter. At that time, we were still just fooling around with the research. We discovered that when people laughed, the hormone system would benefit because laughter prompts good stress (eustress) and decreases bad stress (distress). The reality of wholeness is that each body process has a biological consequence — whether for better or worse. Just like stress can suppress your immune system and lead to sickness, laughter can have the opposite effect by improving and optimizing immune system components and blood flow so you are more "sickness" resistant.

While we may not have started the conversation on health and laughter, our researchers are the leading authority on mirthful laughter and humour, and the psycho-neuro-immunological effects and health benefits they produce.

What are some ways that laughter can affect your physical health?

Laughter causes the release of endorphins, our body's natural painkiller; serotonin, our natural anti-depressant; and good neuropeptides, chemical communicators. It also decreases cortisol, which then reduces stress, lowers blood pressure, increases oxygen intake, enhances the immune system and reduces the risk of having heart disease or a stroke. In healthcare, we often compartmentalize different specialties. We have physiology, biochemistry, endocrinology, and neurology all taught separately, but when we start to look at the whole person, we can see how interconnected the human body really is.

How might laughter affect your mental health?

Laughter triggers the production of key neurochemicals like dopamine, which produce calming, anti-anxiety benefits as well as providing us pleasure and reward. It also increases EEG gamma wave frequency in the brain, which synchronizes brain neurons to help improve your memory and cognitive processing. Laughter has similar benefits as moderate exercise.

Gamma frequency is the highest frequency and is responsible for addressing information processing, improved memory and recall, stress reduction. We now know in neuroscience that gamma frequency enhances the brain's cognitive levels.

In addition to serving as a sort of antidepressant in the brain, laughing can cause a rush of hormones that can make you feel similar positive effects of a narcotic, but unlike opioid drugs, laughter's endorphins are not addictive or damaging to your health.

How long/often should someone laugh to see benefits?

The duration of the laugh is not as important as the reason behind it. Mirthful laughter, as opposed to nervous or embarrassed laughter, promotes the good high-density lipoprotein (HDL) cholesterol and has a cascade of beneficial physiological changes conducive for happiness — happiness being dopamine, serotonin, endorphins. Happiness is the optimal immune system responsivity. Laugh as often and as much as you need until you feel good!

Norman Cousins once wrote, "Of all the gifts bestowed by nature on human beings, hearty laughter must be close to the top." This gift, of both joy and healing, is something that can bring us together and allow us to experience the happiness God longs for us to feel.

Enjoying life and having a lust for laughter is the greatest source of energy available. When people are urged to laugh, they often respond: "There's nothing to laugh about." Life doesn't always give you things to laugh about. You must laugh even when there's nothing to laugh at. Yes, you can laugh at nothing. One can go through simple routines to stimulate laughter. It's hilarious and one can literally feel the extra level of energy generated. Your mind doesn't know the difference. It will produce dopamine, endorphins and immunomodulators, not only in your brain, but throughout your body. Every individual will personally benefit from a renewed burst of energy.

> "I never would have made it if I could not have laughed. It lifted me momentarily out of this horrible situation, just enough to make it livable."
>
> — Viktor Frankl was an Austrian neurologist, psychiatrist, philosopher and Holocaust survivor)

The following practical suggestions, source unknown, offer great ideas on how to live a happy, light-hearted, cheerful life. Practical suggestions that are heard and not practiced are of no use - they must be practiced, must be implemented.

- Get up in the morning with a smile on your face and the words 'good morning, Lord', rather than 'good Lord, it's morning' on your lips. Just doing this will add a new dimension to your life.

- Ensure that your face always wears a smile. Mahatma Gandhi said, "You are not completely dressed until your face wears a smile." It has been said 'wear a smile and you win friends; wear a scowl and you get wrinkles'. Which would you choose?

- Develop a healthy sense of humour. Make sure your humour does not hurt or injure others. A healthy sense of humour is a blessing to oneself as it is a blessing to everyone else. It will save you from many situations. Every great person has had a sense of humour. George Bernard Shaw is such a person: one day, a very beautiful woman met him and said to him, "You have the best intellect in the world, and I have the most beautiful face. If we married, we would be able to produce the perfect child, a child who would have your intellect and my face." Shaw quietly retorted, "Woman, do you realise what would happen to the child if he had your intellect and my face?"

- There's another very amusing story of George Bernard Shaw and GK Chesterton. Shaw was tall and lean. Chesterton was stout and short. When they met each other, Chesterton said to Shaw, "If people looked at you, they would feel that England is under the effect of a famine." Quietly, Shaw answered, "And if they looked at you, they would know the reason."

- You must learn to laugh at yourself. It is very easy to laugh at others, their peculiar points. We must laugh at our own peculiar points; it is only then that we grow a healthy sense of humour. Bishop Fulton John Sheen, famous American Bishop, known for his work on television and radio, relates this incident from his life. One day, he was in a new town, where he had to deliver a lecture at the town hall. He found that it was quite early, so he left the hotel and said he would walk up to the town hall. Not being familiar with the place, he lost his way. He came across a group of little children playing and he asked them,

"Can you show me the way to the town hall?"

One of them volunteered to take him there.

On the way, the little child asked,

"What are you going to do at the town hall?"

The bishop said, "I have to deliver a lecture."

"What is the topic?" asked the child.

Bishop Sheen said, "The topic is 'The Way to the Kingdom of Heaven'."

Immediately, the child began to laugh. He began to laugh hysterically and said, "You don't know the way to the town hall and you are going to tell the people the way to the Kingdom of Heaven?"

We must learn to laugh at ourselves.

- Always look at the bright side of things. Everything has a bright side and a dark side, which is just the less bright side. If we wish to be optimistic, cheerful, happy... we must always see the bright side of life, the bright side of things.

- Never let anyone drive you; always be in the driver's seat. There are so many things that happen to us and we feel hurt, upset or offended. When we feel hurt or offended by something that someone does to us, remember that we are making that person the master of our life. That person drives us. They come and occupy the driver's seat; never let anyone drive you. Let them do and say whatever they like. When we have this attitude towards life, we will always be our own master. Otherwise, we will let others master us, and, once we let others master us, we are being dragged down the road to ill health and sickness.

'Laughter is the sun that drives winter from the human face."

— Victor Hugo

"I have learned never to underestimate the capacity of the human mind and body to regenerate - even when prospects seem most wretched. The life force may be the least understood force on earth."

— Norman Cousins

Every one of us can harness the unlimited power of our mind and body by visualising our goals - by imagining. Visualise your way to success. You can invent your own future. The only limitations are self-imposed. The problem with most of us is that we live according to the expectations of others. We voluntarily forfeit our right to determine our own destiny. Never fall victim to this kind of thinking. We might all be ordinary human beings, but every one of us is capable of doing extraordinary things. Be the sole factor in determining your future. Remember: YOU CAN MAKE THINGS HAPPEN. YOU CAN MAKE THE DIFFERENCE.

"Just as there is no loss of basic energy in the universe, so no thought or action is without its effects, present or ultimate, seen or unseen, felt or unfelt."

— Norman Cousins

Always be positive in your attitude towards life. This has been the teaching of all the great ones. Man is his own friend and man is also his own foe. No one outside you can do you any harm. It is very easy, in difficult and trying circumstances, to throw the blame onto others, to say 'so and so behaved like this towards me; therefore, this is what has happened to me'. No one outside you can do you any harm. You are your own friend; you are your own enemy and you become your friend when you adopt a positive attitude towards life. Expect the very best that life can give you. Expect health instead of sickness. Expect happiness, harmony, prosperity and peace, and the very best will come to you.

Spend some time observing children playing. Notice how frequently they laugh. Research shows that, on average, six-year-olds laugh or giggle 425 times a day, whereas adults laugh only 15 times. Remind yourself of the child in you. Be childlike and less controlled in your life, and allow that inner child to express itself in fun ways.

Let yourself be a little crazy; it lightens up your life. When people ask what you're on, tell them, "I'm on endorphins!"

Live the higher values of life. Values like truth, love, honesty, integrity, co-operation, empathy, respect, humility, freedom, responsibility and unity, and share these with all those whose lives you touch.

If you would like to be happy, make others happy. The happiness that goes out of you will come back to you. Such is the great law. Therefore, do at least one good deed of service every day. Develop a wonderful sense of humour. Laugh and make other people laugh, and you will find that life becomes a festival of joy.

"Each patient carries his own doctor inside him."

— Norman Cousins

Learn to forgive. Researchers in the field of cardio-psycho-neuro-immunology indicate that all the research on heart disease does not make any difference. New research shows that the No. 1 predictor of heart disease is NOT stress/cholesterol/lack of exercise. The No. 1 predictor is an angry, hostile heart. When you hate people (*'I hate that person'*), your heart shrivels up, whereas the heart of the person you hate remains normal, unaffected. You are only hurting yourself. GET RID OF ANGER, HOSTILITY AND HATRED. These are dangerous, corrosive elements as expressed by this powerful analogy: *if you are angry, it is like you are taking poison and expecting the person you're angry with to die.* Learn to forgive. Forgiving, broken down, means FOR GIVING. What? LOVE! A way to forgive is to SEND LOVE. This gets rid of anger.

"The weak can never forgive. Forgiveness is the attribute of the strong."

— Mahatma Gandhi

"Forgiveness is the fragrance that the violet sheds on the heel that has crushed it."

— Mark Twain

How many of you wake up in the morning full of energy and vitality?

There is always an energy exchange between people; there are energy suckers out there - avoid them. They are the cynics, pessimists who say *'yeah, right'* and *'it will never work'* - snivelling at everyone and everything. It takes just one energy sucker to wreck a whole group. We must be energy givers, not suckers.

Never say to anyone *'hi, how are you'* - rather, say *'hi, what's the best thing that's happened to you all day'*.

Ask the question of your neighbour. Ask it of your children. That's how we teach them enthusiasm.

Perhaps the biggest benefit of laughter is that it is free and has no known negative side effects. Humour and laughter are a source of power, healing and survival. We often forget this when caught up in the troubles and trauma of life.

> "Rejoice at your inner powers, for they are the makers of wholeness and holiness in you. Rejoice at seeing the light of day, for seeing makes truth and beauty possible."
>
> — **Hippocrates**

Laughter and Teamwork

A study by recruiting firm, Robert Half International, indicated that 84 of 100 personnel directors and vice presidents from 1, 000 of the nation's largest corporations agreed with this statement: "People with a sense of humour do better at their jobs than those who have little or no sense of humour." And: "People with a sense of humour tend to be more creative, less rigid and more willing to consider and embrace new ideas and methods."

Having a sense of humour at work can not only help to lighten what might be a serious environment, it can also help to defuse difficult situations, reduce stress, create attention for new ideas, build rapport, and help a person be a more approachable and memorable leader. *Start a humour collection.* Stock up on whatever tickles your fancy - humorous videotapes, books, a pair of Groucho Marx glasses or articles by your favourite humour columnists. After a tough day, escape to your humour collection for a quick lift.

- *Have a staff laugh.* Don't hesitate to unwind with your co-workers every now and then with stories of your own personal foibles. Pretty soon, they'll have tales to tell, too.

- *Create a joy list.* Make a list of all your blessings, including people, events and praiseworthy things. Read it at the end of each week.

- *Be playful, imaginative.* Don't squash the child within you. Wear red socks. Buy that nifty remote control red Ferrari you spied in the toy store window. Keep your mind open to silly, irreverent thoughts.

- *Seize the moment.* Don't put off your happiness or your life for a better time; grab a little time each day just for yourself.

- *Let's get real.* This is life. We only have one chance at it. Let's make it enjoyable for ourselves and as many people as we come in contact with.

The best way to cheer yourself is to try to cheer someone else up.

— **Mark Twain**

There was once a man who suffered a severe financial setback. His business failed and he just couldn't land on his feet. He became destitute. Finally, in utter despair, he turned to God. *"Please, God,"* he prayed. *"You've got to help me. Please let me win the lottery."* There was no answer.

The next day was no better, and he prayed again. *"Please, God,"* he urged. *"You've got to do something. The only way I will get back on my feet is if I win the lottery. Make me win."* This went on for a few days. The man thought that God wasn't hearing him. After a while, the man was beyond desperation. With the last breath of hope in his body, he turned to God. *"I beg of you, dear God,"* he said. *"All I need is to win the lottery. It is the only chance I have."* After a moment of silence, a voice came back to him: *"Give me a break. At least buy a ticket."*

Remember that - give yourself a break. At least buy a ticket. We cannot succeed in business or life without performing the right action. We cannot make any sales without having face to face interviews. Act now!

> With the fearful strain that is on me night and day, if I did not laugh I should die.
>
> — Abraham Lincoln

The COVID-19 or coronavirus pandemic is an ongoing global pandemic of coronavirus disease caused by severe acute respiratory syndrome coronavirus 2 (SARS-CoV-2). The novel virus was first identified in the Chinese city of Wuhan in December 2019 and quickly spread around the world. The World Health Organization (WHO) declared a Public Health Emergency of International Concern on 30

January 2020, and a pandemic on 11 March 2020. Multiple variants of the virus have emerged and become dominant in many countries since 2021, with the Alpha, Beta, Gamma, Delta and Omicron variants being the most virulent. According to Johns Hopkins University Coronavirus Resource Center, as of 16 February 2022, more than 415 million cases and 5.84 million deaths have been confirmed, making the pandemic one of the deadliest in history.

Although Covid-19 is by far the worst crisis humanity has confronted in over 100 years, an article by **Richard Schiffman, published in the New York Times Oct. 1, 2020** (updated Oct 2) was titled: **Laughter May Be Effective Medicine for These Trying Times**. It reported that some enlightened doctors, nurses and therapists have a prescription for helping all of us to get through this seemingly never-ending pandemic: **Try a little laughter**.

Humour is not just a distraction from the grim reality of the crisis, said Dr. Michael Miller, a cardiologist at the University of Maryland School of Medicine in Baltimore. It's a winning strategy to stay healthy in the face of it.

"Heightened stress magnifies the risk of cardiovascular events, including heart attacks and strokes," Dr. Miller said. "Having a good sense of humour is an excellent way to relieve stress and anxiety and bring back a sense of normalcy during these turbulent times."

> "Grim care, moroseness, and anxiety—all this rust of life ought to be scoured off by the oil of mirth. Mirth is God's medicine."
>
> **— Henry Ward Beecher**

Laughter releases nitric oxide, a chemical that relaxes blood vessels, reduces blood pressure and decreases clotting, Dr. Miller said. An epidemiological study of older men and women in Japan confirmed that those who tend to laugh more have a lower risk of major cardiovascular illness. Possessing a healthy sense of humour is also associated with living longer, an epidemiological study from Norway reported, although the correlation appears to be stronger for women than for men.

Armed with this growing body of research, Dr. Miller prescribes "one good belly laugh a day" for his patients. It's not just going "ha, ha," he explained, but a "deep physiological laugh that elicits tears of joy and relaxation."

While the long-term impacts of such a practice remain unknown, Sophie Scott, a neuroscientist at University College London, said that laughter has also been shown to reduce the stress hormones cortisol and adrenaline and increases the body's uptake of the feel-good endorphins.

There also appear to be cognitive benefits. Watching a funny video was tied to improvements in short-term memory in older adults and increased their capacity to learn, research conducted by Dr. Gurinder Singh Bains of Loma Linda University found.

Perhaps most relevant today, possessing a sense of humour also helps people remain resilient in the face of adverse circumstances, said George Bonanno, a professor of clinical psychology at Columbia University.

In one study, Dr. Bonanno interviewed young women who had been sexually abused and noted their facial expressions. "Those who managed to laugh or smile at moments during their interview were more likely to be doing better two years later than those who had not," he said. "Humour keeps negative emotions in check and gives us a different perspective, allowing us to see some of the bad things that happen to us as a challenge rather than a threat."

Humour and tragedy may be more intimately connected than one would think.

"Charlie Chaplin once said 'In order to truly laugh you need to be able to take your pain and play with it,'" said Paul Osincup, the president of the Association for Applied and Therapeutic Humour. "Write down all of the most difficult and annoying things about quarantine," Mr. Osincup recommends. "Play with those. See if you can find any humour in your situation."

Megan Werner, a psychotherapist in private practice, uses a similar strategy in her work with at-risk youth in Fayetteville, Ark. During group therapy sessions, she has the teenage gang members she works with interact with "Irwin," a life-size Halloween skeleton, to encourage them to confront their dangerous lifestyle head-on.

"Most of the time you try to deflate a painful situation," she said. "In my therapy work, it's more like 'let's blow it up, let's make it so absurd that we laugh about it.' This releases anxiety, and we're able to approach the topics that weren't approachable initially. It takes the power away from the trauma and helps to defuse it."

Increasingly humour is being integrated into mainstream medical practice with a similar goal, said Dr. Kari Phillips, a resident physician at the Mayo Clinic in Rochester, Minn.

Dr. Phillips observed over a hundred clinical encounters and discovered that humour typically surfaces about twice during a half-hour doctor visit. It is initiated in equal measure by doctors and patients, often to break the ice between them or to help to soften the impact of a difficult medical conversation.

"We found that introducing humour results in better patient satisfaction and empowerment, and it helps people feel more warmth in their connection with the doctor," she said.

Dr. Peter Viccellio, a professor of emergency medicine at Stony Brook University Hospital on Long Island, has seen many Covid-19 patients during his hours in the emergency room. A touch of playfulness and kindly humour, he said, has helped to ease an enormously painful situation for both his patients and members of the overburdened hospital staff.

"Genuine levity can make patients believe that they are not going to meet their doom today" Dr. Viccellio said, but he added that it needs to flow naturally. "If you are empathetic with the person, your humour tends to fit them, it's not forced. If you are not emotionally connected to them and force a joke it can go very wrong."

Some hospitals have initiated formal humour programs, making funny books and videos available and inviting clowns in to interact with their younger patients. Some caregivers are also innovating ways to bring humour into their own practice.

Mary Laskin, a nurse case-manager at Kaiser Permanente in San Diego, has been working with her chronic pain patients online, teaching them laughter exercises alongside practices designed to develop other positive mental states like gratitude and forgiveness.

"This pandemic is like a tiger creeping toward us, a huge slow-motion stressor that makes the experience of pain worse. Humour helps my patients relax and release their grip on pain," she said.

Ms. Laskin suggests that her patients treat humour as a discipline — like physical exercise — that they set aside time for on a daily basis. She recommends "laughter first-aid boxes," where they can stash joke books, funny toys and other props for this purpose.

"Our health care system focuses on passive ways to manage pain like taking a pill or getting an operation," Ms. Laskin said. "I encourage people to actively cultivate the healing power of laughter, which puts them back in the driver's seat."

Humour can also serve to powerfully reaffirm one's humanity in the face of illness or disability, said Dr. B.J. Miller, a palliative care physician in San Francisco who suffered a freak electrical accident in 1990 that cost him two legs and an arm.

After the accident, he said, most people — including medical staff members — viewed him as an object of pity. "There is a solemnity in how people look at you," he said. "You are essentially walled off from others, they stop treating you as a sexual being, they stop treating you as a source of humour."

The one exception, he recalled, were the men who scrubbed off his burned skin in the hospital. "It's a terrible job, I mean you are inflicting reams of pain on someone to save their life," Dr. Miller said. "But this ragtag crew, they were freaking hilarious. One of them had a flask and was drinking during the procedure, they were cracking jokes the whole time."

"It made me stronger because they were looking at me and saying this guy can handle the pain and he can also handle a joke — it made me feel like a human being again."

Inspired by their example, Dr. Miller said, he uses every opportunity to bring a dose of comic relief into his own medical work. Increasingly, he sees his colleagues doing so as well.

"The culture is beginning to shift — injecting humour and humanity back into medicine," he said. "If you can't change what you are dealing with, you can at least change how you view it. Humour gives us the power to do that."

> The art of medicine consists of amusing the patient while nature cures the disease.
>
> — Voltaire (1694 –1778)

Janet M. Gibson, Professor of Cognitive Psychology, Grinnell College, reported as follows in an article in 'The Conversation' in 2020.

Amusement and pleasant surprises – and the laughter they can trigger – add texture to the fabric of daily life.

Those giggles and guffaws can seem like just silly throwaways. But laughter, in response to funny events, actually takes a lot of work, because it activates many areas of the brain: areas that control motor, emotional, cognitive and social processing.

Researchers now appreciate laughter's power to enhance physical and mental well-being.

People begin laughing in infancy, when it helps develop muscles and upper body strength. Laughter is not just breathing. It relies on complex combinations of facial muscles, often involving movement of the eyes, head and shoulders.

Laughter – doing it or observing it – activates multiple regions of the brain: the motor cortex, which controls muscles; the frontal lobe, which helps you understand context; and the limbic system, which modulates positive emotions. Turning all these circuits on strengthens neural connections and helps a healthy brain coordinate its activity.

By activating the neural pathways of emotions like joy and mirth, laughter can improve your mood and make your physical and emotional response to stress less intense. For example, laughing may help control brain levels of the neurotransmitter serotonin, similar to what antidepressants do. By minimizing your brain's responses to threats, it limits the release of neurotransmitters and hormones like cortisol that can wear down your cardiovascular, metabolic and immune systems over time. Laughter's kind of like an antidote to stress, which weakens these systems and increases vulnerability to diseases.

To "get" a joke or humorous situation, you need to be able to see the lighter side of things. You must believe that other possibilities besides the literal exist.

Laughter creates bonds and increases intimacy with others. Linguist Don Nilsen points out that chuckles and belly laughs seldom happen when alone, supporting their strong social role.

Public speakers and comedians try to get a laugh to make audiences feel psychologically closer to them, to create intimacy.

Positive psychology researchers study how people can live meaningful lives and thrive.

Laughter produces positive emotions that lead to this kind of flourishing. These feelings – like amusement, happiness, mirth and joy – build resiliency and increase thinking. They increase subjective well-being and life satisfaction. Researchers find that these positive emotions experienced with humour and laughter correlate with appreciating the meaning of life and help older adults hold a benign view of difficulties they've faced over a lifetime.

You can practice laughing even when alone. Intentionally take a perspective that appreciates the funny side of events.

> When you laugh, aside from the endorphin rush, there's also a spiritual opening. You're not so tight inside yourself. That opening I've found to be a real gift, in people being able to absorb spirituality.
>
> **—Rabbi Sydney Mintz**

In an article in MENTAL HEALTH by Alistair Gardiner on April 30, 2021, a research explains how laughter is the best medicine.

The health benefits of laughing

Crack up. Giggle. Cackle. Guffaw. Chortle. Whatever you want to call it, laughter offers both short- and long-term health benefits, according to the Mayo Clinic. Having a laugh induces immediate physical changes, all of which result in heightened feelings of well-being.

When you laugh, you increase your intake of oxygen-rich air. This stimulates your heart, lungs, and muscles, and prompts the release of endorphins in your brain. Laughing activates and then relieves your body's stress response, and also increases and then lowers your heart rate and blood pressure—all adding up to a calmer feeling. In addition, a good chuckle aids muscle relaxation and can stimulate circulation, both of which can help relieve stress.

As for long-term effects, regular bouts of laughter can improve your immune system, according to medical experts. "When we laugh, it decreases the level of the evil stress hormone cortisol," said Edward Creagan, MD, in an article in *The Seattle Times*. Stressful situations result in a spike in this hormone, which then interferes with the area of the brain that regulates emotions. "When that happens, the immune system deteriorates and becomes washed in a sea of inflammation, which is a factor in heart disease, cancer, and dementia. Cortisol interferes with the body's immune system, putting us at risk for these three groups of diseases," he added.

Positive thoughts and funny experiences, on the other hand, result in the release of neuropeptides, which help fight stress, wrote the Mayo Clinic, adding that regular laughter can also relieve pain and reduce symptoms of depression and anxiety.

> "In the sweetness of friendship let there be laughter, and sharing of pleasures. For in the dew of little things the heart finds its morning and is refreshed."
>
> — Khalil Gibran

Laughter is also associated with living longer for other reasons, according to Dr. Creagan. Being funny or enjoying comedy is usually an attractive trait, and research indicates that social connectedness is a factor that contributes to longevity.

This link between laughing and longevity is also supported by some evidence. One study, published in *Psychosomatic Medicine*, looked at the association between humour and survival in patients with all-cause mortality, and mortality due to cardiovascular diseases (CVD), infections, cancer, and chronic obstructive pulmonary diseases. Researchers studied a cohort of approximately 54,000 individuals over a 15-year period.

They found that having a good sense of humour is positively associated with survival from CVD-related mortality in women and with infection-related mortality in individuals of any gender. Researchers concluded this was due to laughter's effect as "a health-protecting cognitive coping resource." They measured this factor by asking participants to estimate their ability to find a funny element in any given situation; those with higher scores on this question tended to live longer.

> Against the assault of laughter, nothing can stand.
>
> — Mark Twain

The following poem gives further reasons to bring laughter into our lives.

SOLITUDE - ELLA WHEELER WILCOX

Laugh, and the world laughs with you;
Weep, and you weep alone.
For the sad old earth must borrow its mirth,
But has trouble enough of its own.
Sing, and the hills will answer;
Sigh, it is lost on the air.
The echoes bound to a joyful sound,
But shrink from voicing care.

Rejoice, and men will seek you;
Grieve, and they turn and go.
They want full measure of all your pleasure,
But they do not need your woe.
Be glad, and your friends are many;
Be sad, and you lose them all.
There are none to decline your nectared wine,
But alone you must drink life's gall.

Feast, and your halls are crowded;
Fast, and the world goes by.
Succeed and give, and it helps you live,
But no man can help you die.
There is room in the halls of pleasure
For a long and lordly train,
But one by one we must all file on
Through the narrow aisles of pain.

ELLA WHEELER WILCOX

Lucy Rayfield, PhD, Lecturer at the University of Bristol, spent much of her career studying laughter and comedy. She studied Italian comedy and its reception in 16th-century France, the political consequences of laughter in the Wars of Religion, and the historical antecedents to today's main theories of humour. Her research into laughter started with a PhD at the University of Oxford.

In an article in *The Conversation on May 28, 2021,* she states that most of us have needed a good laugh since the onset of the Covid-19 pandemic. Searches on Netflix for horror dipped at the peak of the first lockdown, while stand-up comedy saw a huge jump in viewers. I quote from the article below, in her own words.

Much of her research has revealed fascinating things about how humour appeals to us in times of hardship. But the pandemic has really amplified the roles that comedy can play and brought home our reliance on humour.

Our need to laugh in the face of disaster is by no means new. In ancient Rome, gladiators would leave humorous graffiti on barrack walls before going to their deaths. The ancient Greeks also sought new ways to laugh at deadly disease. And during the Black Death pandemic in 1348, the Italian Giovanni Boccaccio wrote the Decameron, a collection of often funny tales told by storytellers isolating from the plague.

The need to avoid offence with humour is just as ancient. In 335 BCE, Aristotle advised against laughing at anything painful or destructive. The Roman educator Quintilian also outlined in 95 CE the very fine line between *ridere* (laughter) and *deridere* (derision). It's still generally accepted a common position that humour shouldn't hurt, and this is particularly true when the object of laughter is already vulnerable.

When the boundary between laughter and derision is respected, comedy can play a key role in helping us to recover from disaster, providing benefits which explain our tendency to seek humour in serious situations, especially in terms of enhancing our sense of physical and mental wellbeing.

Laughter serves as a great workout (laughing 100 times burns as many calories as 15 minutes on an exercise bike), helping to relax our muscles and promote circulation. Combinations of exercise and laughter — such as the increasingly popular "laughter yoga" — can also provide significant benefits to patients with depression.

Laughter also decreases stress hormones and increases endorphins. In tough times, when we have thousands of thoughts a day, a bout of giggling provides our brains with respite we desperately need.

In the same way, we seek humour in a crisis because it is difficult to feel scared and amused at the same time, and most often, the combination of these emotions result in feeling thrill and not terror.

Sigmund Freud explored this in 1905 when revising the so-called "relief theory", suggesting that laughter feels good because it purges our system of pent-up energy. Even in the 1400s, clerics argued that mirth was vital for keeping up spirits, explaining that people are like old barrels which explode if they aren't uncorked from time to time.

As levels of loneliness reached a record high during the winter lockdown (in November 2020, one in four UK adults reported feeling lonely), laughter has also been crucial in bringing people together. Not only is it typically a communal activity – some scientists believe that our human ancestors laughed in groups before they could speak – it's even more contagious than yawning.

Given that we're far more likely to laugh at topics we find personally relatable, humour has helped people to identify with one another during lockdowns. This in turn creates a sense of unity and solidarity, alleviating our sense of disconnectedness. Literature scholar and author Gina Barreca maintains that "laughing together is as close as you can get without touching".

The most wasted of all days is one without laughter.

— E E Cummings

Laughter can also be a means of easing our worries. Joking around a fear, especially during a pandemic, can make it more manageable, a phenomenon known by comedians as "finding the funny". Joking about a virus heightens our sense of power over it and relieves anxiety. Joking can also be useful because it enables us to talk about our problems and to express fears we may otherwise find hard to put into words.

Though many of us have felt guilty for seeking humour in the pandemic, let's not add this to our list of worries. Certainly, our situation may not always be a laughing matter. But laughing itself matters, and when used appropriately, it can be one of our most effective coping mechanisms during a crisis, allowing us to find a healthier balance with others, with ourselves, and even with events beyond our control."

> Laughter serves as a blocking agent. Like a bulletproof vest, it may help protect you against the ravages of negative emotions that can assault you in disease.
>
> — Norman Cousins

FIFTEEN

SELF-MANAGEMENT IS LIFE MANAGEMENT

"A man's mind may be likened to a garden, which may be intelligently cultivated or allowed to run wild; but whether cultivated or neglected, it must, and will, bring forth. If no useful seeds are put into it, then an abundance of useless weed seeds will fall therein, and will continue to produce their kind."

— James Allen

Before getting into 'Self-Management is Life Management', we need to discuss a most common term, 'time management'.

What is time management? A common complaint in the workplace is that there's not enough time. How do we manage our time?

You can never manage time. Time exists: there are 24 hours or 1, 440 minutes in the day, and the 86, 400 seconds every day will pass on; nobody can change that or manage it in any way. Therefore, time management is actually work management - managing our work in the given time!

We try all types of methods to be able to do this, such as hiring a personal assistant, trying to work more efficiently, drawing up 'to do' lists and so on. However, when you look back at the end of the day, how many items are ticked off? Why? You need to ask the next question: if the work needs to be managed in the allotted time, who is it that has to manage it? *You*! If you yourself are not managed, it's not possible to do this.

Therefore, time management = work management = self-management. Let's park this and look at what life consists of. Life comprises two elements: **you** - the individual, and the **world** - people and objects. When you contact the world, there is an experience. The flow of experiences is life. Modern scientists have worked to make the world a better place to live in, and to make people more comfortable and happy. They have done an amazing job, radically improving everything around us. However, in spite of all the advancements, human beings are not at peace. People are infested with stress and strain, worry and anxiety. People are less happy today than they were 30, 50 or 100 years ago! Why? While science has improved one aspect of an experience i.e. the **world**, the second component of an experience i.e. the individual, **you** - has been neglected to a fault. This omission has resulted in a host of problems, setbacks and suffering that inflict and afflict humanity.

ALL MANAGEMENT IN THE WORLD BOILS DOWN TO SELF-MANAGEMENT. You manage yourself; you manage your life and the world.

What does that mean? First, we need to know and understand who *you* are. What are the elements that make up every human being?

Spirit and Matter

A human being comprises Spirit and matter. Spirit is also known as the highest Self, the God principle within. It is that which enlivens us to function - to perceive and act, to feel and to think. Matter, in turn, is comprised of three elements - body, mind and intellect. When spirit and matter meet, there is a scintillating expression of life through the individual.

Let us examine the specific roles of the body, mind and intellect.

> "People are anxious to improve their circumstances,
> But are unwilling to improve themselves;
> They therefore remain bound."

— James Allen

Body, Mind and Intellect

Body is the outer personality. It is what you see when you meet me; what I see when I meet you. It drives the personality from experience to experience, just like the car that transports you from place to place. It is the gross part of our personality.

There's something propelling it. When I write, it's an action. When you read, that's an action. Something other than the body drives us to act, and the question is… what is driving the body to action?

When you make a decision to go to a certain place, does your body decide to go there? No, there is an inner personality, the driver. The inner personality is made up of two entities: the **mind** and the **intellect**. Both of these are made up of thoughts. However, there is a distinction between the two. The mind is made up of indiscriminate thoughts, while the intellect is made up of discriminate thoughts.

It's critical for us to know the difference between the mind and intellect so that we understand what's driving us. The mind is that which houses our emotions, feelings, likes and dislikes, desires, impulses, worries of the past and anxieties for the future, etc.

Beyond the mind is the intellect. This is hardly known. People only understand intelligence. There's no programme in the world to develop the intellect - it's not taught at schools or universities. Intellect is that which thinks, reasons, judges and decides, as opposed to the mind with its feelings and emotions.

The following analogies may help illustrate the difference.

Mind is the water flowing in a river; intellect is the river banks.

Mind is like a child; intellect is like an adult.

Are you operating on the impulse and emotion of the mind, or reason and judgment of the intellect?

This choice is of utmost importance; it makes all the difference. Only human beings are provided with an intellect. No other creature has it. Animals don't need an intellect. Observe the animal kingdom. They are perfect. They are programmed from birth to death. No animal is overweight or underweight. All creatures have the perfect weight. Their eating habits are perfect. They have the perfect mating habits. Every aspect of their lives is perfect. A tiger cannot become a vegetarian. That's its nature. A cow cannot become a meat eater.

However, look at human beings. People are constantly battling with weight, dietary and other issues.

Human beings don't have a pre-programmed existence; we have the **choice of action**. Therefore, we are given an intellect to choose, to reach perfection in all aspects of our lives.

Without this, we are living under the whims and fancies of the mind - emotionally, impulsively.

The proportion - or ratio - of use of one's mind to intellect determines the type of individual that one is.

So the question is: on what basis do we make choices? We *have* to know!

We are in trouble because we operate at the level of the mind. As human beings, we need to act on intellect. It's the only way. Human beings do *not* have a pre-programmed existence; we have the *choice of action* - because we have this amazing equipment called the **intellect**.

How the mind and intellect impact our actions is best explained in this example. You offer a sweet to a diabetic. The mind says 'take it'; the intellect says 'no'. What does he choose? It depends on which is stronger - his mind or his intellect! This is the scary reality. We are not able to choose in favour of our better judgment because we are victims of our mind. We can't even blame anyone, because we are not taught how to do this.

Offer a child the choice between candy in one hand and a wad of $100 notes in the other - he will choose the candy. Why? Because the intellect is not developed!

That's exactly what we adults are choosing every day of our lives – candy, in other forms, such as name, fame, money, possessions, titles and so forth, and we miss the essentials of life. Why? Because the mind is too strong and the intellect is very weak!

Most people's lives are governed by the likes and dislikes of the mind instead of by reason and judgment of the intellect. We do what we like and do not do what we don't like, even though what we don't like might be good for us.

Our likes and dislikes have been fed since we were born. Then our friends cater to our likes and dislikes, and then we grow up and get married and each partner feeds the other partner's likes and dislikes. We function more on likes and dislikes today than on reason and discrimination.

Unfortunately, what we like often turns out to be negative, eventually, and what we dislike often turns out to be positive. "What is like poison at the beginning becomes nectar at the end and what is like nectar at the beginning becomes poison at the end." (the essence of verses 37 and 38 of the *Bhagavad Gita*, Chapter 18)

Here is an example: you decided last night to exercise at 6 a.m. this morning... but you didn't. What happened? Snooze button? How many of you faced that choice this morning? What about junk food versus healthy food? Do we give in to anger, greed or jealousy? These are all emotions of the mind. There is no intellectual supervision.

People end up ruining their lives, partners, children and businesses. Giant companies like Lehman Brothers closed down. The 2008 financial crisis threatened to bring down the world's economy. If not for government bail-outs, who knows where the world economy would be now. The reason for the turmoil is that a miniscule number of people, including some of the most powerful global leaders, are operating at the level of the intellect. Greed and avarice - at the level of the mind - have consumed most people.

If left to its own whims and fancies, the mind can create havoc... it can destroy you.

We cannot operate at the level of the mind. We must reason about the right thing to do and do it. Everyone follows a 'herd instinct', because the intellect is not available.

Intellect is not the same as intelligence! We need to distinguish between these two words. Most people confuse intellect with intelligence. There's a fundamental difference. Intelligence is obtained from external sources - schools and universities, teachers and textbooks - to gain knowledge to make a living, whether it be in finance, engineering, medicine, law, or any other occupation, for that matter.

Intellect, on the other hand, is internal. It is the ability to think, reason, judge and decide. Thinking is an art, a skill, a technique that has to be learnt and practiced, just like playing chess or golf. Other than governing the mind, the intellect is also needed to use the intelligence we have acquired.

Despite our modern comforts, most people are still not happy. This is due to the fact that they follow the 'herd instinct'. They can't or don't manage their lives using their intellect. Examples can be found of brilliant scientists and world leaders who are known to smoke and drink excessively, and to suffer from stress and strain. They have all the intelligence, but virtually zero intellect.

Not only is the intellect required to govern and control the mind, it is also a necessary tool for fully utilising the intelligence you have acquired. For example, millions have studied medicine, but just one person, Edward Jenner, developed a cure for smallpox in 1796. There have been numerous major medical breakthroughs since, such as Sir Alexander Fleming's discovery of penicillin in 1928, Jonas Salk's cure for Polio in 1955, and Dr Chris Barnard's first human heart transplant in 1967. Individuals such as these used their intellects. One individual thought of the Panama Canal, the Egyptian Pyramids, the Chunnel linking England and France, or the Great Wall of China, has resulted in these outstanding engineering feats, achieved only through use of the intellect.

Going back in time, further examples of the use of the intellect were apparent. Aryabhata (476–550 CE) from India was the first of the major mathematicians-astronomers-physicists and the author of several treatises on these subjects. The place-value system, first seen in the 3rd-century Bakhshali Manuscript, was clearly in place in his work, although he did not use a symbol for zero.

It was the Indian mathematician Brahmagupta (628 A.D.) who used zero as a number for the first time. The brilliant mathematicians of Ancient Greece, so far ahead of their time in many ways, had not been able to make this breakthrough. Neither had anyone else, until Brahmagupta came along!

It was a huge conceptual leap to see that zero is a number in its own right, the cornerstone of modern mathematics and physics, plus the spin-off technology. Marcus du Sautoy, a professor of mathematics at the University of Oxford, said, "Today we take it for granted that the concept of zero is used across the globe and is a key building block of the digital world. But the creation of zero as a number in its own right, which evolved from the placeholder dot symbol found in the Bakhshali manuscript, was one of the greatest breakthroughs in the history of mathematics. We now know that it was as early as the third century that mathematicians in India planted the seed of the idea that would later become so fundamental to the modern world. The findings show how vibrant mathematics have been in the Indian sub-continent for centuries."

Even **Albert Einstein** acknowledged this when he declared, "We owe a lot to the Indians, who taught us how to count, without which no worthwhile scientific discovery could have been made."

One can have all the intelligence in the world, but it is critical to understand and use the intellect.

> "We are thinking beings, and we cannot exclude the intellect from participating in any of our functions."
>
> — **William James**

How do we develop the intellect? Never take anything for granted. Always question everything!

Most of us take everything for granted. We must question every aspect of life, for example: why do I need a degree? A job? A business? Marriage? Children? It is not that one should not engage in these things, but we need to think and deliberate on them before making a decision, understanding the impact and potential consequences of any decision we *do* make.

It is the utilisation of our intellect that impacts our life. An ungoverned mind = an ungoverned life. Therefore, self-management = life management. You manage yourself, you manage your life!

When we change our focus from the external to the internal - understanding the powerful equipment that we have at our disposal - and make a conscious effort to develop our intellects, we will experience a state of peace and happiness.

As renowned German philosopher, Arthur Schopenhauer, stated:

"It is difficult to find happiness within oneself, but it is impossible to find it anywhere else."

Never should you let your present happiness be determined by future acquisition. If you do, the happiness you seek will be elusive and you will remain in a permanent state of unhappiness.

> "You have the Heaven within you, the paradise, the home of bliss within you, and yet you are searching for pleasures in objects in the streets, searching for that thing outside, outside in the objects of the senses. How strange!"
>
> — **Swami Rama Tirtha**

SIXTEEN

UNIQUE PURPOSE IN LIFE

"At the centre of your being
you have the answer;
you know who you are
and you know what you want."

— Loa Tzu

Each one of us has a unique talent and a unique way of expressing it. There is something that we can do better than anyone else in the whole world. There is a reason we are here, and we have to find out what that reason is. What we must focus on is asking ourselves how we unfold our essential Being, our *true* nature and how we can serve humanity. The challenge for each one of us is to identify what our unique purpose in life is, and then to pro-actively set out to convert it to reality. In so doing, each one of us can make a significant contribution to the upliftment of our fellow beings. We *can* make a difference. We *can* make our country - and indeed the world - a better place for all of us. But it all starts with changing ourselves first. We must live, love, laugh, learn and leave a legacy.

In the words of George Bernard Shaw: "This is the true joy in life... being used for a purpose recognised by yourself as a mighty one... being a force of nature instead of a feverish selfish little clod of ailments and grievances complaining that the world will not devote itself to making you happy... I am of the opinion that my life belongs to the whole community and as long as I live it is my privilege to do for it whatever I can. I want to be thoroughly used up before I die. For the harder I work the more I live. I rejoice in life for its own sake. Life is no brief candle to me. It's a sort of splendid torch which I've got to hold up for the moment and I want to make it burn as brightly as possible before handing it on to future generations."

> "Knowing others is intelligence;
> knowing yourself is true wisdom.
> Mastering others is strength;
> mastering yourself is true power."
>
> — Lao Tzu, Tao Te Ching

The Secret of Success

With all its worship of material success, society has missed a fundamental and profound truth: success depends on *who we are*, not what we say or do, not on our qualifications or bank balance, not on our position or status, and certainly not on how we dress, the car we drive or the kind of house we live in. No matter how successful we appear to be on the outside, we will remain unfulfilled unless we nurture the seeds of divinity inside us. As discussed below, the great sages of the East have declared from time immemorial that our essential nature is divine. Many Western philosophers also say the same thing. *All major religions* pronounce this emphatically.

Old Testament:	**I am That I am**
New Testament:	**The Kingdom of God is Within**
Quran:	**The most excellent Jihad is that for the Conquest of Self**
Bhagavad Gita:	**I am the Self in all Beings**
Upanishads:	**Self is God**

> "We have come into this exquisite world to experience ever and ever more deeply our divine courage, freedom and light!"
>
> — **Hafez (also known as Hafiz) – 14th Century Persian Poet**

Purpose of Life:

In the final analysis, **the purpose of life is a life of purpose**.

Every human being is seeking one thing and one thing only–happiness. Most people continuously pursue external objects and beings, with the express purpose of obtaining happiness, pleasure or satisfaction. Invariably, this happiness lasts only for a short while, yet we continue this fruitless pursuit. It seems as if we are trying to fill an imaginary void within us and we believe external acquisition can fill this void. But it never does. The great sages and saints have been preaching for thousands of years that what we are seeking, can never be found in the world. The direction of our search has to change to within. All the answers and solutions we ever seek are to be found inside us. These masters declare emphatically that, at the deepest core of our beings, we are complete, fulfilled, peaceful and blissful – *paripoorna* all-full in Sanskrit. At that core level, we are all the same – the one undivided Self. And we are all seeking the very same thing. Everything we do, we do for that reason alone.

What is it that we are seeking? Everlasting Happiness. Permanent Bliss. Eternal Peace. These are all synonyms. This exalted state can be achieved only when we reach the ultimate of human perfection – the highest, truest, noblest expression of our Self. It doesn't matter what we do. Whether one is a chef, a plumber, an engineer, a doctor or whatever, the essential reason one is doing that is to be happy. We may say the main reason is to earn a living, to support our family. Of course it is, but why do we want to do that? If we keep asking *why*, the final answer will be for happiness. We marry? Why? For happiness. We take a vacation. Why? For happiness. Another person smokes a cigarette. Why? Ultimate reason is happiness. Why does this search for happiness go on perpetually? Because that's our original nature – pure bliss, pure happiness. Consciously or unconsciously, that's what we are seeking.

> "Live your life as though your every act were to become a universal law."
>
> **— Immanuel Kant**

Don't be defined by what others say, feel or think about you. Your self-worth must not, and cannot, be defined by others. You are the master of your own destiny. You construct your future or you destroy your future. Every experience, every crisis, every difficulty, every tragedy, all the joyful and sorrowful things you've ever been through are silently, relentlessly drawing you to your highest Self. You may not know it at the time.

The opposite of spirituality is worldliness. Worldliness is more than money, position, status, power, etc. Worldliness is believing that we can achieve ultimate peace and happiness and can resolve all our inner conflicts by looking for solutions in the external world. That if we change things externally, all our internal problems will be resolved. There is zero evidence to support this contention. No one can ever gain real, lasting peace and happiness by changing things outside of themselves. What is required is a complete change in the direction of our pursuit. The only real solution to resolving inner conflicts and attaining permanent peace and happiness is to go within.

One has to be grounded and follow some spiritual practice to succeed in the world. By success we do not mean material wealth only. One can be the richest person in the world and still be bored and miserable. The fundamental lesson is that spirituality is not a journey in time, neither is it a journey in space, but it is a journey from ignorance to knowledge – from ignorance of our real nature to knowledge of our original Nature - a state of pure, unconditioned Consciousness. The purpose of human existence is to unveil one's infinite nature.

> "Each one has to find his peace from within. And peace, to be real, must be unaffected by outside circumstances."
>
> — **Mahatma Gandhi**

We can undertake this profound journey to Self-discovery wherever we are. In my case, I made a conscious, deliberate, transformative decision to relocate to the home of spirituality, India. I needed some structure, a tried and tested program to methodically, systematically, scientifically study the ancient scriptures in contemporary thought and language. This I found in a small village in India called Malavli, 108 kilometres from Mumbai, where the Vedanta Academy is situated. Established in 1988, the Academy has been imparting this profound knowledge of Vedanta to youngsters from all parts of the world through the medium of a structured three-year residential course. The founder, guru and head lecturer of the Academy is a world-renowned philosopher, Swami A Parthasarathy who is currently 94 years old.

The word 'life-changing' is used pretty liberally, but for me, the decision to relocate to another country was indeed so. It was uplifting and illuminating. Our daily routine – 7 days a week, 365 days a year is getting up at 4:00 am for self-study. 4:00 – 6:00 am is regarded as the most conducive time to study and reflect on the higher values of life. The rest of each day is made up of yoga, sport, lectures, small and big group discussions, work on the campus, meals, community singing, etc. Interacting with young students from ages 17 – 35 is fascinating. I enjoy playing table tennis and soccer with these youngsters to this day. We have a great jogging track around the Academy and other games played here are cricket, basketball, volleyball, badminton and frisbee.

> "We must not cease from exploration, and the end of all our exploring will be to arrive where we began and to know the place for the first time."
>
> — T.S. Eliot

Bhagavad Gita:

We delve deep into Vedanta, a knowledge that has been handed down from the enlightened masters in the Himalayas thousands of years ago. One of the key scriptural texts that I studied in-depth in the three-year residential course is the *Bhagavad Gita*, an illuminating book that has influenced many philosophers, thinkers, actors, musicians and others in the east and west, including Mahatma Gandhi, Aldous Huxley, Henry David Thoreau, Ralph Waldo Emerson, Carl Jung, Hermann Hesse, George Harrison, Will Smith, etc. Some tributes to the Gita:

- Aldous Huxley, the English philosopher and writer found *Gita* "the most systematic statement of spiritual evolution of endowing value to mankind." He also felt, *Gita* is "one of the most clear and comprehensive summaries of perennial philosophy ever revealed; hence its enduring value is subject not only to India but to all of humanity."

- J. Robert Oppenheimer, American physicist and director of the Manhattan Project, learned Sanskrit in 1933 and read the *Bhagavad Gita* in the original form, citing it later as "one of the most influential books to shape my philosophy of life".

- Henry David Thoreau wrote "In the morning I bathe my intellect in the stupendous and cosmogonal philosophy of the *Bhagavad Gita* in comparison with which our modern world and its literature seem puny and trivial."

- Ralph Waldo Emerson said this about the *Bhagavad Gita*: "I owed a magnificent day to the *Bhagavad Gita*. It was as if an empire spoke to us, nothing small or unworthy, but large, serene, consistent, the voice of an old intelligence which in another age and climate had pondered and thus disposed of the same questions which exercise us."

- Hollywood actor Will Smith, who starred in numerous blockbuster films, including *Independence Day* and *Men in Black*, and who Forbes named the most bankable star in the world in 2013, has been intensely studying the *Bhagavad Gita* over the past year. "I fell in love with the *Bhagavad Gita*", he said. On a visit to India a few years ago he commented on the *Gita*: "To be reading that and to be here... my inner Arjuna is being channelled."

"I wish I could show you when you are lonely or in darkness, the astonishing light of your own being."

— Hafez

The *Bhagavad Gita* declares emphatically that the purpose of life is to realize one's essential, original Nature, to unveil the immaculate Self within, thus attaining spiritual Enlightenment. The *Gita* is the philosophic portion of the great epic Mahabharata and covers the rivalry between two royal families, the Pandavas, comprising five righteous, honourable brothers and their cousins, the Kauravas, made up of one hundred unrighteous, evil brothers. Through trickery and evil means, the Kauravas dispossessed the Pandavas of their kingdom and possessions and sent them into exile for thirteen years, during which time the Kauravas ruled the kingdom. The Pandavas were promised a return of their kingdom after their exile. When they completed their exile and claimed back their kingdom, the head of the Kauravas, Durydhona, declined to adhere to the terms of the agreement. In spite of numerous efforts to mediate, he refused to give up any part of the kingdom, thus making battle inevitable. Full preparations were thus made for a war between the royal cousins and their respective armies.

The Pandava commander, Prince Arjuna, who was renowned as one of the greatest archers and warriors at that time, asked Lord Krishna, his charioteer, to place the chariot between the two armies so that he could see the fighters on the opposing side. When he saw his guru, grandfather, uncles, cousins, nephews and other close family and friends, he was overwhelmed by emotions, mentally devastated and intellectually immobilized. The valiant warrior could not fight as his mind was distressed with sorrow. He put aside his bow and arrow and surrendered to Lord Krsna for guidance. This is when the Lord delivered the sermon of the *Bhagavad Gita* to Arjuna.

Lord Krishna skilfully, systematically and scientifically resurrects and revitalizes the famed warrior Arjuna with a higher purpose. The profound lessons that he imparts to Arjuna are of immense significance and benefit to the whole of humanity. They are as relevant today as they were thousands of years ago.

> "People travel to wonder
> at the height of the mountains,
> at the huge waves of the seas,
> at the long course of the rivers,
> at the vast compass of the ocean,
> at the circular motion of the stars,
> and yet they pass by themselves
> without wondering. "
>
> — SAINT AUGUSTINE

Essential Life Lessons from the *Bhagavad Gita*:

- Perform perfect action and success is a natural outcome. Perfect action is action dedicated to a higher ideal, devoid of any self-interest, ego and attachment.

- The quality of an action is determined by the quality of the intention backing the action. Therefore, a pure action is that which is performed with unselfish, noble intentions, while an impure action is that which is performed with selfish, ignoble intentions.

- It is the obligation of every human being to improve the inner condition of their mind and not the outer condition of the world. In fact, it is through inner transformation that the entire world benefits and becomes purified.

- Every human being must take time daily to listen, read and reflect on the higher truths of life. It is only through this exercise that you become rooted in your own personality. When your roots are deep and strong, you remain firm and unmoving.

- A human being alone is gifted with an intellect, *buddhi* in Sanskrit. The intellect is the capacity to think, reason, judge and decide. The intellect alone can control and direct the emotions and impulses of the mind, leading the personality towards its higher purpose.

- A true human being is one who lives in the world, but is never affected by the world. You must live your life like a lotus leaf in water. A lotus leaf is born, lives and dies in water, but due to its waxy cuticle, water never enters the leaf, it is never wet. So too, you are born, live and will die in the world, but you must never let the world enter your being. The higher knowledge of

Vedanta develops the intellect. The intellect is your armour. It protects you from the onslaughts of the world.

• The quintessence of spirituality is renunciation. Renunciation is commonly misunderstood to mean giving up your possessions, titles, wealth, relationships etc. Renunciation has nothing to do with giving up anything. In fact, renunciation is the process of taking up higher values of life, gaining higher knowledge in life. As you rise with knowledge, the earlier values that you had, start to drop away. This is the natural process of growth, just as when a child grows into a teenager, he develops a fascination for gadgets and games and completely forgets about his toys and trinkets.

Every single human being is Divine. Our mission in life is to recognise our Divinity. We will never find fulfilment until we reach our original state of Godhood, a state of infinite Bliss. Thus our ultimate goal in life is to unveil our essential Being, to become Self-Enlightened.

We can only share with others to the extent that we have unfolded our highest Self. If we do not fill ourselves with higher knowledge, we will not have anything to share. Take the example of a lake. Once a lake is full, does it have to advertise this fact? No, absolutely not. People and animals will make their way to the lake to draw water. So, once we are full of Self-knowledge, people will be knocking on our door to seek this from us. The foundation of success is knowing who we are, where we come from and the purpose of our life. So our principal obligation is to align our personality with our core purpose, and the only duty we have is to work on ourselves.

"There is only one corner of the universe you can be certain of improving, and that's your own self."

— **Aldous Huxley**

A Vedic verse declares: "The inner intelligence of the body is the ultimate and supreme genius in nature. It mirrors the wisdom of the cosmos." This genius is inside each of us, a part of our inner blueprint that cannot be erased. The divine intention is for every human being to enjoy unlimited success and it therefore follows that success is supremely natural.

"Remember that when you leave this earth, you can take with you nothing that you have received - only what you have given: a full heart, enriched by honest service, love, sacrifice and courage."

— **St. Francis of Assisi**

The most popular American poet of his day, former Professor at Harvard College, Henry Wadsworth Longfellow (February 27, 1807 – March 24, 1882), penned the following beautiful poem. He was inspired to write this after a heartfelt conversation he had with a friend and fellow Harvard professor; the two had spent an evening 'talking of matters that lie near one's soul – and how to bear one's self doughtily in life's battle and make the best of things'. The next day, Longfellow wrote A *Psalm of Life*, which contains some profound observations glorifying life and its possibilities. It is an invocation to mankind to follow the path of righteousness. It is full of meaning and purpose and will enrich our lives if we apply the profound lessons contained therein.

A PSALM OF LIFE

TELL me not, in mournful numbers,
    Life is but an empty dream!
For the soul is dead that slumbers,
    And things are not what they seem.

Life is real! Life is earnest!
    And the grave is not its goal;
Dust thou art, to dust returnest,
    Was not spoken of the soul.

Not enjoyment, and not sorrow,
    Is our destined end or way;
But to act, that each tomorrow
    Find us farther than today.

Art is long, and time is fleeting,
    And our hearts, though stout and brave,
Still, like muffled drums, are beating
    Funeral marches to the grave.

In the world's broad field of battle,
    In the bivouac of life,
Be not like dumb, driven cattle!
    Be a hero in the strife!

Trust no future, howe'er pleasant!
    Let the dead past bury its dead!
Act - act in the living present!
    Heart within, and God o'er head!

Lives of great men all remind us
    We can make our lives sublime,
And, departing, leave behind us
    Footprints on the sands of time;

Footprints, that perhaps another,
   Sailing o'er life's solemn main,
A forlorn and shipwrecked brother,
   Seeing, shall take heart again.

Let us, then, be up and doing,
   With a heart for any fate;
Still achieving, still pursuing,
   Learn to labour and to wait.

HENRY WADSWORTH LONGFELLOW

We will ultimately be judged by the legacy we leave to future generations. What did we do to make this world a better place? It all starts with oneself. As Mahatma Gandhi so eloquently and succinctly declared: "Be the change that you wish to see in the world."

> "When you are dead, seek for your resting place not in the earth, but in the hearts of men."
>
> — Rūmī

It is the impact, the contribution and the positive difference we make in the lives of others, the extent to which we live a life of generosity, gratitude, love, selflessness, service and sacrifice, the degree to which we have fortified ourselves with higher knowledge and the eternal truths of life, and our level of Self-unfoldment that counts in the final analysis. Live your life with purpose!

> "And you? When will you begin that long journey into yourself?"
>
> — Rumi

SEVENTEEN

REFLECTIONS ON LIFE AND LIVING

"The fountain of content must spring up in the mind, and he who hath so little knowledge of human nature as to seek happiness by changing anything but his own disposition, will waste his life in fruitless efforts and multiply the grief he proposes to remove."

— **Samuel Johnson**

Throughout life, I have been in search of something beyond what life appeared to be superficially. This led to me exploring various 'spiritual' avenues, which I engaged in for many years. After a while, I came to the realization that these 'paths' were not an end in themselves but a means to an end. A good friend asked if I would like to attend talks on the *Bhagavad Gita*. I was still 'exploring,' as it were, and decided to attend the first lecture at the Exhibition Centre in central Durban in August 2001, with around fifty people in attendance.

Sunandaji, daughter-disciple of Swami Parthasarathy, world-renowned philosopher and founder of the Vedanta Academy in Pune, India, commenced the discourse. Her eloquent, logical, scientific exposition of the sacred text was incredible and I was instantly 'hooked'. It was so enchanting that I took Sussie and our three daughters the next day. Swami Parthasarathy was scheduled to do a Retreat at a Drakensburg Hotel that weekend, from Friday afternoon to Sunday. I attended with Sarisha and Linestha. It was captivating and illuminating. Half way through the Retreat, we were all so enthralled with this profound knowledge of life and living that the girls made the momentous decision to enrol for the three-year residential course in Vedanta Philosophy at the Vedanta Academy in Pune, India. Linestha completed her final high school exams and Sarisha her undergraduate degree at the end of 2001 and joined the Academy in January 2002.

Vedanta is a philosophy which enunciates the eternal principles of life and living. It is a scientific system of principles that governs human life. Living is an art, a skill, a technique that has to be learned and practiced. Few have understood this throughout the span of human history. This process of learning is not taught at schools or universities, nor in moral or religious institutions. People thus go through a mechanical way of living merely following a routine set by their predecessors. They lack this fundamental knowledge of living and become victims of stress and strain.

> "Everything has been figured out,
> Except how to live.
>
> — Jean Paul Sartre

The Vedanta Academy offers three-year residential courses on Vedanta philosophy. It is unique in its purpose and design and was established to assist young individuals to develop their intellects through a systematic programme of study and reflection, encouraging questioning and enquiry. This revolutionary method of education facilitates the development of the intellect and does not merely provide intelligence on a subject.

Sarisha continues to study at the Academy and propagate the knowledge. After 7 years of study at the Academy, Linestha returned to South Africa to teach the philosophy, first in Durban for a few years and thereafter in Johannesburg. After 11 years in South Africa, she then relocated to Pune, India at the end of 2020 to continue studying and propagating the knowledge. Sussie, Nevita and I regularly visited and attended lectures at this learning institution since the girls joined in 2002.

In February 2015, after an extensive study in music, my youngest daughter Nevita made the decision to enrol for the three-year residential course at the Academy, thoroughly enjoying its liberal approach to education. She graduated in 2018.

"The unexamined life is not worth living."

— Socrates

After intense deliberation, and considering the essential nature of these profound teachings, I enrolled for the three-year residential course at the Academy. Sussie and I left South Africa in March 2016 and relocated to Pune, India. I commenced my course on 31 March, graduating in 2019.

"The essence of philosophy is that a man should so live that his happiness shall depend as little as possible on external things."

— Epictetus

"The great blessings of mankind are within us and within our reach; but we shut our eyes, and like people in the dark, we fall foul upon the very thing we search for, without finding it."

— Seneca (7 BC to 65 AD)

"Knowing yourself is the beginning of all wisdom."

— Aristotle

On reflecting over the last two decades – the past six years specifically, I'd like to share some of the many profound lessons learned.

Ultimate Mission

- As mentioned earlier, the fundamental lesson is that spirituality is not a journey in time, neither is it a journey in space, but it is a journey from ignorance to knowledge – from ignorance of our real nature to knowledge of our original Nature - a state of pure, unconditioned Consciousness.

- So, as all the great scriptural texts and sages declare, the ultimate purpose of life is to regain our original Nature, to become Enlightened, Self-realized, to be in a state of absolute, permanent peace and bliss.

- Beyond the body, mind and intellect, beyond the waking, dream and deep-sleep states is the Self, which one must unfold.

- The Self or God-Principle in me is the same in you and every living being. Thus, at the deepest core of our beings, we are all the same – pure Divinity, the very Source of all power, happiness, peace and bliss.

- In his discourses in the USA and elsewhere, the great Indian Sage Swami Rama Tirtha always addressed his audiences as "My own Self in the form of Ladies and Gentlemen." He saw and felt God in all names and forms. See the Self in all living beings.

- Learn to look beyond people's physical attributes and identify with their inner Self, which is the same in all of us. There are many rivers, but one ocean. Similarly, there are billions of humans, but one Self, present in every being. There's a profound Sanskrit saying: *Ya pasyati sa pasyati* – he who sees, sees.

"You have no need to travel anywhere - journey within yourself. Enter a mine of rubies and bathe in the splendour of your own light."

— **Rūmī**

"We have within ourselves enough to fill the present day with joy, and overspread the future years with hope."

— **William Wordsworth**

Higher Ideal

- Set higher ideals in life. As one takes up higher ideals, and gets established in them, the lower ideals fall off.

- The higher the ideal in life, the greater the initiative to work.

"Be not anxious as to the reward of your labours; mind not the future; think not of success and failure. Work for work's sake. Work is its own reward. Without dejection at the past and without anxiety as to the future - work, work, work in the living present. This spirit will keep you cheerful under all circumstances."

— **Swami Rama Tirtha**

Developing the Intellect

- The fundamental requirement for a stress-free life is to develop a strong intellect to control desires.

- There are two ways to develop the intellect.

  o Question everything

  o Never take anything for granted

- Purify your emotions. Ensure they are guided by your intellect.

- All decisions ought to be made on the basis of logic and reason and not feeling, emotion, impulse, like or dislike.

- Embark on this study of life and living which provides the Manual of Life - the essential instructions on how to conduct yourselves and how to navigate the challenges of the world.

"It is better to conquer yourself than to win a thousand battles. Then the victory is yours. It cannot be taken from you, not by angels or by demons, heaven or hell."

— Gautama Buddha

Right Action & Success

- Success is an effect. The cause is 'right action'.

- Do what you ought to do in life and do not be concerned with results.

- A paradox of life is that what is pleasant in the beginning is often unpleasant in the end and what is unpleasant in the beginning is often pleasant in the end.

- Life is to give, not to take. Be a giver.

- Live a life of service and sacrifice.

- Follow the 3 C SUCCESS formula:

  o Concentration – the intellect holding the mind on the present action without allowing it to slip into the past or future.

  o Consistency – the intellect directing all actions towards the chosen ideal.

  o Cooperative Endeavour – developing the support and cooperation of others related to your work.

"If you want to awaken all of humanity, then awaken all of yourself. If you want to eliminate the suffering in the world, then eliminate all that is dark and negative in yourself. Truly, the greatest gift you have to give is that of your own self-transformation."

— Lao Tzu

"The highest education is that which does not merely give us information, but makes our life in harmony with all existence."

— Rabindranath Tagore

Stress:

- People believe that factors outside of themselves cause stress. Stress is entirely an internal phenomenon.

- Stress is nothing but mental agitation caused by unfulfilled desires. Uncontrolled desires create havoc.

- Pleasure or pain, joy or sorrow, peace or stress are not found in external objects or beings but in how you relate to them.

"No matter what happens, it is within my power to turn it to my advantage."

— Epictetus

Correct understanding of Life

- Understand what is Permanent and what is temporary, fleeting, transient. We tend to give an exaggerated value to objects and beings of the world, all of which are impermanent, ephemeral, passing and have a shelf life. Only the Self within meets the test of Reality and is Eternal, All-pervading, Permanent.

- In the final analysis, we take nothing physical or material when we pass on. The only thing we take is the higher knowledge we have gained.

- The great sage Rama Tirtha implores us to rise from idle dreams and take to incessant work to win the freedom which is the fruit, not of conquest over others, but over one's self.

- Knowledge is always accompanied by humility.

- Drop the notion of 'I' and 'my', 'me' and 'mine' in all transactions of life.

- Always be objective. Maintain an impersonal, detached attitude in life.

- Each individual has a distinct role to play in this world.

- Learn to look at persons, beings and things, environments and situations, as what they are and not what you would like them to be.

- To maintain perfect relationships:

  o Properly assess the world – people, environment and things. You will then have right expectations and not meet with disappointment.

  o No confrontation - avoid unnecessary confrontation with the world.

- Be the example you want others to follow.

- Never let your present happiness be dependent on future acquisition.

- You are poor when your desires exceed your wealth. You are rich when your desires are contained within your wealth.

"Be content with what you have;
rejoice in the way things are.
When you realise there is nothing lacking,
the whole world belongs to you."

— Lao Tzu

"Nothing is enough for the man to whom enough is too little."

— Epicurus

In his profound essay on Self-Reliance, Ralph Waldo Emerson's recurrent themes are the need for each individual to avoid conformity and false consistency and do what they think is right, no matter what others think. Published first in 1841 in Essays, "Self-Reliance" took shape over a long period of time. Emerson writes that self-sufficiency gives one the freedom one needs to unfold one's true self and attain true independence. He believed that individualism, personal responsibility and nonconformity were essential to a thriving society.

> "Let man lift himself by himself, let him not lower himself; his self alone is his friend, his self alone is his enemy."

> — *Bhagavad Gita* **Chapter 6 Verse 5**

Spirituality, specifically the idea that truth is within one's self, is a recurring theme in Emerson's essay. Emerson mentions that *"nothing has authority over the self"*. Emerson's essay focuses and consistently relates back to one major theme: *"Trust thyself"*. The idea of believing in one's self and one's worth is the main theme in the essay. Emerson posits that reliance upon institutionalized religion hinders the ability to grow mentally as an individual.

Solitude and the community appear within the essay many times. Emerson writes how the community is a distraction to self-growth and advocates more time being spent reflecting on one's self. He mentions *"but the great man is he who in the midst of the crowd keeps with perfect sweetness the independence of solitude,"* and emphasizes, *"Nothing can bring you peace but yourself."*

Two powerful extracts from Self-Reliance are quoted below:

> *"Ne te quaesiveris extra."* (Do not seek for things outside of yourself)

> "Man is his own star; and the soul that can
> Render an honest and a perfect man,
> Commands all light, all influence, all fate;

Nothing to him falls early or too late.
Our acts our angels are, or good or ill,
Our fatal shadows that walk by us still."

— Epilogue to Beaumont and Fletcher's Honest Man's Fortune

"These are the voices which we hear in solitude, but they grow faint and inaudible as we enter into the world. Society everywhere is in conspiracy against the manhood of every one of its members. Society is a joint-stock company, in which the members agree, for the better securing of his bread to each shareholder, to surrender the liberty and culture of the eater. The virtue in most request is conformity. Self-reliance is its aversion. It loves not realities and creators, but names and customs.

Whoso would be a man must be a nonconformist. He who would gather immortal palms must not be hindered by the name of goodness, but must explore if it be goodness. Nothing is at last sacred but the integrity of your own mind."

— Ralph Waldo Emerson, Self-Reliance

"The mind is its own place, and in itself can make a heaven of hell, a hell of heaven."

— John Milton, Paradise Lost

EIGHTEEN

INSPIRATIONAL POEMS AND STORIES

This chapter contains a number of profound poems and stories. Poetry is described as a language of the heart, often conveying deep philosophical messages that have the ability to transform and enrich our lives.

Poetry may make us from time to time a little more aware of the deeper, unnamed feelings which form the substratum of our being, to which we rarely penetrate; for our lives are mostly a constant evasion of ourselves.

— T. S. Eliot

A few poems below, interspersed among the stories, are from one of my all-time favourite books, *The Prophet*, by Lebanese poet/philosopher, Kahlil Gibran (January 6, 1883 – April 10, 1931). Gibran was born in Lebanon and immigrated to the United States at age two with his mother and siblings. *The Prophet* was first published in the United States in 1923 and has since become one of the best-selling books of all time, having been translated into more than 100 languages.

KAHLIL GIBRAN ON SELF-KNOWLEDGE

Your hearts know in silence the secrets of the days and the nights.
But your ears thirst for the sound of your heart's knowledge.
You would know in words that which you have always known in thought.
You would touch with your fingers the naked body of your dreams.

And it is well you should.
The hidden well-spring of your soul must needs rise and run murmuring to the sea;
And the treasure of your infinite depths would be revealed to your eyes.
But let there be no scales to weigh your unknown treasure;
And seek not the depths of your knowledge with staff or sounding line.
For self is a sea boundless and measureless.

Say not, "I have found the truth," but rather, "I have found a truth."
Say not, "I have found the path of the soul."
Say rather, "I have met the soul walking upon my path."
For the soul walks upon all paths.
The soul walks not upon a line, neither does it grow like a reed.
The soul unfolds itself, like a lotus of countless petals.

KAHLIL GIBRAN

INVICTUS: BY WILLIAM ERNEST HENLEY

Invictus, meaning "unconquerable" or "undefeated" in Latin, is a poem about courage in the face of death and holding on to one's dignity despite the indignities life places before us.

Background:

At the age of 12, Henley contracted tuberculosis of the bone. A few years later, the disease progressed to his foot, and physicians announced that the only way to save his life was to amputate directly below the knee. It was amputated when he was 17. Despite his disability, he survived with one foot intact and led an active life until his death at the age of 53.

During Henley's twenty-month ordeal between 1873 and 1875 at the Royal Edinburgh Infirmary in Scotland, he wrote "Invictus" and other poems. This poem was written shortly after his leg was amputated.

The Poem

Out of the night that covers me,
　　Black as the pit from pole to pole,
I thank whatever gods may be
　　For my unconquerable soul.

In the fell clutch of circumstance
   I have not winced nor cried aloud.
Under the bludgeonings of chance
   My head is bloody, but unbowed.

Beyond this place of wrath and tears
   Looms but the Horror of the shade,
And yet the menace of the years
   Finds and shall find me unafraid.

It matters not how strait the gate,
   How charged with punishments the scroll,
I am the master of my fate,
   I am the captain of my soul.

WILLIAM ERNEST HENLEY

The following poem, *Be Alive* by Jan Michaelson, was recited at an MDRT Annual Meeting. It encapsulates how to add humour, meaning and joy to our daily lives.

Be Alive, think freely, smile often
Tell those you love that you do,
Rediscover old friends,
Make new ones

Hope, grow, give, give in,
Pick some daisies, share them,
Keep a promise.

Laugh heartily, reach out, let someone in,
Hug a kid, slow down.
See a sunrise, listen to rain,
Trust life, have faith, enjoy,

Make some mistakes, learn from them.
Explore the unknown,
Celebrate life,
Be alive.

JAN MICHAELSON

KAHLIL GIBRAN ON LOVE (EXTRACTS)

"Love gives naught but itself and takes
naught but from itself.
Love possesses not nor would it be
possessed;
For love is sufficient unto love.

When you love you should not say,
'God is in my heart', but, rather, 'I am
in the heart of God'.
And think not you can direct the course
of love, for love, if it finds you worthy,
directs your course.

Love has no other desire but to fulfil
itself.
But if you love and must needs have
desires, let these be your desires:
To melt and be like a running brook
that sings its melody to the night.
To know the pain of too much tenderness.
To be wounded by your own under-
standing of love;
And to bleed willingly and joyfully.
To wake at dawn with a winged heart
and give thanks for another day of loving;
To rest at the noon hour and meditate
love's ecstasy;
To return home at eventide with gratitude;
And then to sleep with a prayer for the
beloved in your heart and a song of praise
upon your lips."

KAHLIL GIBRAN

One should not be unduly affected by events and circumstances, especially when these are beyond our control. It is important to maintain objectivity at all times and understand that nothing lasts forever. This applies to whatever we experience, whether good or bad, wealth or poverty, joy or sorrow, pain or pleasure. The following poem encapsulates this detached attitude wonderfully:

EVEN THIS SHALL PASS AWAY BY THEODORE TILTON

Once in Persia reigned a king,
Who upon his signet ring
Graved a maxim true and wise,
Which, if held before his eyes,
Gave him counsel at a glance
Fit for every change and chance.
Solemn words, and these are they;
"Even this shall pass away."

Trains of camels through the sand
Brought him gems from Samarcand;
Fleets of galleys through the seas
Brought him pearls to match with these;
But he counted not his gain
Treasures of the mine or main;
"What is wealth?" the king would say;
"Even this shall pass away."

'Mid the revels of his court,
At the zenith of his sport,
When the palms of all his guests
Burned with clapping at his jests,
He, amid his figs and wine,
Cried, "O loving friends of mine;
Pleasures come, but do not stay;
'Even this shall pass away.'"

Lady, fairest ever seen,
Was the bride he crowned the queen.
Pillowed on his marriage bed,
Softly to his soul he said:
"Though no bridegroom ever pressed
Fairer bosom to his breast,
Mortal flesh must come to clay –
Even this shall pass away."

Fighting on a furious field,
Once a javelin pierced his shield;
Soldiers, with a loud lament,
Bore him bleeding to his tent.
Groaning from his tortured side,
"Pain is hard to bear," he cried;
"But with patience, day by day,
Even this shall pass away."

Towering in the public square,
Twenty cubits in the air,
Rose his statue, carved in stone.
Then the king, disguised, unknown,
Stood before his sculptured name,
Musing meekly: "What is fame?
Fame is but a slow decay;
Even this shall pass away."

Struck with palsy, sore and old,
Waiting at the Gates of Gold,
Said he with his dying breath,
"Life is done, but what is Death?"
Then, in answer to the king,
Fell a sunbeam on his ring,
Showing by a heavenly ray,
"Even this shall pass away."

THEODORE TILTON

Below is one of William Shakespeare's most famous love sonnets.

SONNET 116: LET ME NOT TO THE MARRIAGE OF TRUE MINDS

Let me not to the marriage of true minds
Admit impediments. Love is not love
Which alters when it alteration finds,
Or bends with the remover to remove.
O no! it is an ever-fixed mark
That looks on tempests and is never shaken;
It is the star to every wand'ring bark,
Whose worth's unknown, although his height be taken.
Love's not Time's fool, though rosy lips and cheeks
Within his bending sickle's compass come;
Love alters not with his brief hours and weeks,
But bears it out even to the edge of doom.
If this be error and upon me prov'd,
I never writ, nor no man ever lov'd.

WILLIAM SHAKESPEARE

This sonnet attempts to define love, by telling both what it is and is not. In the first quatrain, the speaker says that love – "the marriage of true minds" - is perfect and unchanging; it does not "admit impediments," and it does not change when it finds changes in the loved one. In the second quatrain, the speaker tells what love is through a metaphor: a guiding star to lost ships ("wand'ring barks") that is not susceptible to storms (it "looks on tempests and is never shaken"). In the third quatrain, the speaker again describes what love is not: it is not susceptible to time. Though beauty fades in time as rosy lips and cheeks come within "his bending sickle's compass," love does not change with hours and weeks: instead, it "bears it out even to the edge of doom." In the couplet, the speaker attests to his certainty that love is as he says: if his statements can be proved to be error, he declares, he must never have written a word, and no man can ever have been in love." (Credit to *sparknotes.com* for this explanation)

"Robert Frost wrote 'The Road Not Taken' as a joke for a friend, the poet Edward Thomas. When they went walking together, Thomas was chronically indecisive about which road they ought to take and—in retrospect—often lamented that they should, in fact, have taken the other one. Soon after writing the poem in 1915, Frost griped to Thomas that he had read the poem to an audience of college students and that it had been "taken pretty seriously ... despite doing my best to make it obvious by my manner that I was fooling. ... Mea culpa." However, Frost liked to quip, "I'm never more serious than when joking." As his joke unfolds, Frost creates a multiplicity of meanings, never quite allowing one to supplant the other—even as 'The Road Not Taken' describes how choice is inevitable."

— Katherine Robinson

THE ROAD NOT TAKEN: BY ROBERT FROST

Two roads diverged in a yellow wood,
And sorry I could not travel both
And be one traveller, long I stood
And looked down one as far as I could
To where it bent in the undergrowth;

Then took the other, as just as fair,
And having perhaps the better claim,
Because it was grassy and wanted wear;
Though as for that the passing there
Had worn them really about the same,

And both that morning equally lay
In leaves no step had trodden black.
Oh, I kept the first for another day!

Yet knowing how way leads on to way,
I doubted if I should ever come back.

I shall be telling this with a sigh
Somewhere ages and ages hence:
Two roads diverged in a wood, and I—
I took the one less travelled by,
And that has made all the difference.

ROBERT FROST

KAHLIL GIBRAN ON MARRIAGE

"You were born together, and together you shall be forevermore.
You shall be together when white wings of death scatter your
days.
Aye, you shall be together even in the silent memory of God.
But let there be spaces in your togetherness,
And let the winds of the heavens dance between you.

Love one another, but make not a bond of love:
Let it rather be a moving sea between the shores of your souls.
Fill each other's cup, but drink not from one cup.
Give one another of your bread, but eat not from the same loaf.
Sing and dance together and be joyous, but let each one of you be
alone,
Even as the strings of a lute are alone though they quiver with the same
music.

Give your hearts, but not into each other's keeping.
For only the hand of life can contain your hearts.
And stand together, yet not too near together:
For the pillars of the temple stand apart,
And the oak tree and the cypress grow not in each other's
shadow."

KAHLIL GIBRAN

WE ARE ALL MADE TO FLY

Once there was a king who received a gift of two magnificent falcons from Arabia. They were peregrine falcons, the most beautiful birds he had ever seen. He gave the precious birds to his head falconer to be trained.

Months passed and, one day, the head falconer informed the king that, though one of the falcons was flying majestically, soaring high in the sky, the other bird had not moved from its branch since the day it had arrived.

The king summoned healers and sorcerers from all the land to tend to the falcon, but no one could make the bird fly. He presented the task to the members of his court, but, the next day, the king saw through the palace window that the bird had still not moved from its perch. Having tried everything else, the king thought, maybe I need someone more familiar with the countryside to understand the nature of this problem. So he cried out to his court, "Go and get a farmer."

In the morning, the king was thrilled to see the falcon soaring high above the palace gardens. He said to his court, "Bring me the doer of this miracle."

The court quickly located the farmer, who came and stood before the king. The king asked him, "How did you make the falcon fly?"

With his head bowed, the farmer said to the king, "It was very easy, Your Highness. I simply cut the branch where the bird was sitting."

We are all made to fly - to realise our incredible potential as human beings. But, instead of doing that, we sit on our branches, clinging to the things that are familiar to us. The possibilities are endless, but, for most of us, they remain undiscovered. We conform to the familiar, the comfortable, the mundane. So, for the most part, our lives are mediocre instead of exciting, thrilling and fulfilling.

So let us learn to destroy the branch of fear we cling to and free ourselves to the glory of flight.

- FROM THE BOOK WHY WALK WHEN YOU CAN FLY BY ISHA JUDD

KAHLIL GIBRAN ON CHILDREN

"Your children are not your children.
They are the sons and daughters of Life's longing for itself.
They come through you, but not from you,
And though they are with you, yet they belong not to you.

You may give them your love, but not your thoughts.
For they have their own thoughts.
You may house their bodies, but not their souls,
For their souls dwell in the house of tomorrow, which you cannot
visit, not even in your dreams.
You may strive to be like them, but seek not to make them like
you.
For life goes not backward nor tarries with yesterday.

You are the bows from which your children as living arrows are
sent forth.
The archer sees the mark upon the path of the infinite, and He
bends you with His might that His arrows may go swift and far.
Let your bending in the archer's hand be for gladness;
For even as he loves the arrow that flies, so He loves also the bow
that is stable."

KAHLIL GIBRAN

Dr. Howard Kelly (1858-1943) was a distinguished physician who was one of the four founding doctors of Johns Hopkins, the first medical research university in the U.S. and arguably one of the finest hospitals anywhere. In 1895 he established the department of Gynaecology and Obstetrics at that school. Over the course of his career, he advanced the sciences of gynaecology and surgery, both as a teacher and as a practitioner.

According to Dr Kelly's biographer, Audrey Davis, the doctor was on a walking trip through Northern Pennsylvania one spring day when he stopped by a farm house for a drink of cool spring water. A little girl answered his knock at the door and, instead of water, brought him a glass of fresh milk. After a short friendly visit, he went on his way. Some years later, that same little girl came to him for an operation. Just before she left for home, her bill was brought into the room and across its face was written in a bold hand, "Paid in full with one glass of milk."

How often were you totally certain that you knew something, as if it was the absolutely truth, only to realise later that you were completely wrong – as in the poem *The Cookie Thief* below? I am sure every one of us has had this experience at one time or another. What if our assumptions are incorrect and we arrive at these wrong conclusions on a regular basis? We thus need to challenge some of our most fundamental beliefs, examine and analyse them carefully and rationally, subject them to interrogation, experiment with them, and, if they agree with reason and cause no harm, accept and live by them.

This is succinctly captured in the following quote:

> "The trouble with most folks isn't their ignorance. It's knowin' so many things that aint so."
>
> — Josh Billings

The following poem illustrates the danger of assuming something or labelling others, without establishing the facts.

THE COOKIE THIEF

A woman was waiting at an airport one night
With several long hours before her flight
She hunted for a book in the airport shop
Bought a bag of cookies and found a place to drop
She was engrossed in her book, but happened to see
That the man beside her as bold as could be
Grabbed a cookie or two from the bag between
Which she tried to ignore to avoid a scene

She munched cookies and watched the clock
As this gutsy cookie thief diminished her stock
She was getting more irritated as the minutes ticked by
Thinking, 'If I wasn't so nice I'd blacken his eye'

With each cookie she took, he took one too
And when only one was left she wondered what he'd do
With a smile on his face and a nervous laugh
He took the last cookie and broke it in half

He offered her half as he ate the other
She snatched it from him and thought, 'Oh brother
This guy has some nerve and he's also rude
Why he didn't even show any gratitude'
She had never known when she had been so galled
And sighed with relief when her flight was called
She gathered her belongings and headed for the gate
Refusing to look back at the thieving ingrate

She boarded the plane and sank in her seat
Then sought her book, which was almost complete
As she reached in her baggage she gasped with surprise
There was her bag of cookies in front of her eyes
'If mine are here,' she moaned with despair
'Then the others were his and he tried to share'
'Too late to apologise,' she realised with grief
That she was the rude one, the ingrate, the thief.

VALERIE COX

KAHLIL GIBRAN ON TEACHING

No man can reveal to you aught but that which already lies half asleep in the dawning of your knowledge.

The teacher who walks in the shadow of the temple, among his followers, gives not of his wisdom but rather of his faith and his lovingness.

If he is indeed wise he does not bid you enter the house of his wisdom, but rather leads you to the threshold of your own mind.

The astronomer may speak to you of his understanding of space, but he cannot give you his understanding.

The musician may sing to you of the rhythm which is in all space, but he cannot give you the ear which arrests the rhythm nor the voice that echoes it.

And he who is versed in the science of numbers can tell of the regions of weight and measure, but he cannot conduct you thither.

For the vision of one man lends not its wings to another man.

And even as each one of you stands alone in God's knowledge, so must each one of you be alone in his knowledge of God and in his understanding of the earth.

KAHLIL GIBRAN

The following poem teaches us humility.

THE INDISPENSABLE MAN

Sometime when you're feeling important;
Sometime when your ego's in bloom;
Sometime when you take it for granted,
You're the best qualified in the room:
Sometime when you feel that your going,
Would leave an unfillable hole,
Just follow these simple instructions,
And see how they humble your soul.

Take a bucket and fill it with water,
Put your hand in it up to the wrist,
Pull it out and the hole that's remaining,
Is a measure of how much you'll be missed.
You can splash all you wish when you enter,
You may stir up the water galore,
But stop, and you'll find that in no time,
It looks quite the same as before.

The moral of this quaint example,
Is to do just the best that you can,
Be proud of yourself, but remember,
There's no indispensable man.

SAXON WHITE KESSINGER

KAHLIL GIBRAN ON WORK

You work that you may keep pace with the earth and the soul of the earth.
For to be idle is to become a stranger unto the seasons, and to step out of life's procession, that marches in majesty and proud submission towards the infinite.

When you work you are a flute through whose heart the whispering of the hours turns to music.
Which of you would be a reed, dumb and silent, when all else sings together in unison?

Always you have been told that work is a curse and labour a misfortune.
But I say to you that when you work you fulfil a part of earth's furthest dream, assigned to you when that dream was born,
And in keeping yourself with labour you are in truth loving life,
And to love life through labour is to be intimate with life's inmost secret.

But if you in your pain call birth an affliction and the support of the flesh a curse written upon your brow, then I answer that naught but the sweat of your brow shall wash away that which is written.

You have been told also life is darkness, and in your weariness you echo what was said by the weary.
And I say that life is indeed darkness save when there is urge,
And all urge is blind save when there is knowledge,
And all knowledge is vain save when there is work,
And all work is empty save when there is love;
And when you work with love you bind yourself to yourself, and to one another, and to God.

And what is it to work with love?
It is to weave the cloth with threads drawn from your heart, even as if your beloved were to wear that cloth.

It is to build a house with affection, even as if your beloved were
to dwell in that house.

It is to sow seeds with tenderness and reap the harvest with joy,
even as if your beloved were to eat the fruit.

It is to charge all things you fashion with a breath of your own
spirit.

Work is love made visible.

And if you cannot work with love but only with distaste, it is
better that you should leave your work and sit at the gate of the
temple and take alms of those who work with joy.

For if you bake bread with indifference, you bake a bitter bread
that feeds but half man's hunger.

And if you grudge the crushing of the grapes, your grudge distils
a poison in the wine.

And if you sing though as angels, and love not the singing, you
muffle man's ears to the voices of the day and the voices of the
night.

KAHLIL GIBRAN

THE MOST BEAUTIFUL FLOWER

The park bench was deserted as I sat down to read.
Beneath the long, straggly branches of an old willow tree.
Disillusioned by life with good reason to frown,
For the world was intent on dragging me down.

And if that weren't enough to ruin my day,
A young boy out of breath approached me, all tired from play.
He stood right before me with his head tilted down
And said with great excitement, "Look what I found!"

In his hand was a flower, and what a pitiful sight,
With its petals all worn - not enough rain, or too little light.
Wanting him to take his dead flower and go off to play,
I faked a small smile and then shifted away.

But instead of retreating he sat next to my side
And placed the flower to his nose
And declared with overacted surprise,
"It sure smells pretty and it's beautiful, too.

That's why I picked it; here, it's for you."
The weed before me was dying or dead.
Not vibrant of colours: orange, yellow or red.
But I knew I must take it, or he might never leave.

So I reached for the flower, and replied, "Just what I need."
But instead of him placing the flower in my hand,
He held it mid-air without reason or plan.
It was then that I noticed for the very first time

That weed-toting boy could not see: he was blind.
I heard my voice quiver; tears shone in the sun
As I thanked him for picking the very best one.
"You're welcome." He smiled, and then ran off to play.

Cheryl Costello-Forshey

KAHLIL GIBRAN ON JOY AND SORROW

Your joy is your sorrow unmasked.
And the selfsame well from which your laughter rises was
oftentimes filled with your tears.
And how else can it be?
The deeper that sorrow carves into your being, the more joy you can
contain.
Is not the cup that holds your wine the very cup that was burnt
in the potter's oven?
And is not the lute that soothes your spirit, the very wood that
was hollowed with knives?
When you are joyous, look deep into your heart and you shall
find it is only that which has given you sorrow that is giving you
joy.
When you are sorrowful look again in your heart, and you shall
see that in truth you are weeping for that which has been your
delight.

Some of you say, "Joy is greater than sorrow," and others say,
"Nay, sorrow is the greater."
But I say unto you, they are inseparable.
Together they come, and when one sits alone with you at your
board, remember that the other is asleep upon your bed.

Verily you are suspended like scales between your sorrow and
your joy.
Only when you are empty are you at standstill and balanced.
When the treasure-keeper lifts you to weigh his gold and his
silver, needs must your joy or your sorrow rise or fall.

KAHLIL GIBRAN

In the final analysis, the profound words and lessons contained
in each of the above poems has the potential to make a lasting
and significant positive impact on our lives.

NINETEEN

PHILOSOPHICAL QUOTES

Meaningful quotations by Eastern and Western thinkers/authors/ philosophers are fascinating. Enjoy some of my favourite quotes:

"Creating without claiming. Doing without taking credit. Guiding without interfering. This is primal virtue."

— Lao Tzu

"The ideal man bears the accidents of life with dignity and grace, making the best of circumstances."

— Aristotle

"What you seek is seeking you."

— Rumi

"Self-sufficiency is the greatest of all wealth."

— Epicurus

"To expect the unexpected shows a thoroughly modern intellect."

— Oscar Wilde

"What lies behind us and what lies before us are tiny matters compared to what lies within us."

— Henry Stanley Haskins

"If thou wilt make a man happy, add not unto his riches but take away from his desires."

— Epicurus

"I sit on a man's back choking him and making him carry me, and yet assure myself and others that I am sorry for him and wish to lighten his load by all means possible... except by getting off his back."

— Leo Tolstoy

"It is better for you to be free of fear lying upon a pallet, than to have a golden couch and a rich table and be full of trouble."

— Epicurus

"The mind that is anxious about future events is miserable."

— Seneca

"I've decided to be happy because it's good for my health."

— Voltaire

"Self-control is strength. Right thought is mastery. Calmness is power."

— James Allen

"Pay bad people with your goodness; fight their hatred with your kindness. Even if you do not achieve victory over other people, you will conquer yourself."

— Leo Tolstoy

"Silence is one of the hardest kind of arguments to refute. There is no good substitute for wisdom; but silence is the best that has yet been discovered."

— Josh Billings

"Those who can make you believe absurdities, can make you commit atrocities."

— Voltaire

"Life has no meaning a priori... It is up to you to give it a meaning, and value is nothing but the meaning that you choose."

— Jean-Paul Sartre

"Keep silence for the most part, and speak only when you must, and then briefly."

— Epictetus

"It is not the length of life, but the depth of life."

— Ralph Waldo Emerson

"What you do speaks so loudly that I cannot hear what you say."

— Ralph Waldo Emerson

"When you learn, teach. When you get, give."

— Maya Angelou

"Wherever there is a human being, there exists the opportunity for an act of kindness."

— Seneca, Dialogues and Essays

"The Moving Finger writes; and, having writ,
Moves on: nor all thy Piety nor Wit
Shall lure it back to cancel half a Line,
Nor all thy Tears wash out a Word of it."

— Omar Khayyam

"He prayeth best who loveth best,;
Both man and bird, and beast.
He prayeth well who loveth well,
All things both great and small."

— Samuel Taylor Coleridge

Honour and shame from no condition rise;
Act well your part, there all the honor lies.

— Alexander Pope

"To understand the actual world as it is,
Not as we should wish it to be,
Is the beginning of wisdom."

— Bertrand Russell

"The greatest wealth is to live content with little."

— Plato

"We are not rich by what we possess
But by what we can do without."

— **Immanuel Kant**

"A man is rich in proportion to the number of things which he can afford to let alone."

— **Henry David Thoreau, Walden**

"It is not work that kills men; it is worry. Work is healthy; you can hardly put more upon a man than he can bear. Worry is the rust upon the blade. It is not the revolution which destroys the machinery but the friction. Fear secretes acids; but love and trust are sweet juices."

— **Henry Ward Beecher**

"A noble and God-like character is not a thing of favor or chance, but is the natural result of continued effort in right thinking, the effect of long-cherished association with God-like thoughts."

— **James Allen, As a Man Thinketh**

"Everything can be taken from a man or a woman but one thing: the last of human freedoms - to choose one's attitude in any given set of circumstances, to choose one's own way."

— **Viktor E. Frankl**

"Do not spoil what you have by desiring what you have not; remember that what you now have was once among the things you only hoped for."

— **Epicurus**

"God has entrusted me with myself. No man is free who is not master of himself. A man should so live that his happiness shall depend as little as possible on external things. The world turns aside to let any man pass who knows where he is going."

— Epictetus

"Many people die with their music still in them. Why is this so? Too often, it is because they are always getting ready to live. Before they know it, time runs out."

— Oliver Wendell Holmes

"No one saves us but ourselves. No one can and no one may. We ourselves must walk the path."

— Gautama Buddha

'Gratitude is not only the greatest of virtues, but the parent of all others.'

— Marcus Tullius Cicero

"The nakedness of the indigent world may be clothed from the trimmings of the vain."

— Oliver Goldsmith

"What the mind of man can conceive and believe, IT CAN ACHIEVE!"

— Napoleon Hill

"Our scientific power has outrun our spiritual power. We have guided missiles and misguided men."

— Martin Luther King, Jr.

"It is not in the stars to hold our destiny but in ourselves."

— Shakespeare

"There is so much good in the worst of us,
And so much bad in the best of us,
That it hardly behooves any of us
To talk about the rest of us."

— Edward Wallis Hoch

The things you really need are few and easy to come by; but the things you can imagine you need are infinite, and you will never be satisfied.

— Epicurus

"Just as one candle lights another and can light thousands of other candles, so one heart illuminates another heart and can illuminate thousands of other hearts."

— Leo Tolstoy

"To live is the rarest thing in the world. Most people exist, that is all."

— Oscar Wilde

"The flower that blooms in adversity is the rarest and most beautiful of all."

— Walt Disney

"When you realize how perfect everything is you will tilt your head back and laugh at the sky."

— Buddha

"In three words I can sum up everything I've learned about life: it goes on."

— Robert Frost

"Even after all this time the sun never says to the earth, 'You owe me.' Look what happens with a love like that. It lights the whole sky."

— Hafez (also known as Hafiz)

"Let us rise up and be thankful, for if we didn't learn a lot today, at least we learnt a little, and if we didn't learn a little, at least we didn't get sick, and if we got sick, at least we didn't die; so, let us all be thankful."

— Gautama Buddha

"Remember, no human condition is ever permanent. Then you will not be overjoyed in good fortune or too scornful in misfortune."

— Socrates

"Life consists not in holding good cards but in playing those you hold well."

— Josh Billings

"To be yourself in a world that is constantly trying to make you something else is the greatest accomplishment."

— Ralph Waldo Emerson

"If you think about disaster, you will get it. Brood about death and you hasten your demise. Think positively and masterfully, with confidence and faith, and life becomes more secure, more fraught with action, richer in achievement and experience."

— Swami Vivekananda

"We don't laugh because we're happy, we are happy because we laugh."

— **William James**

"So when you are listening to somebody, completely, attentively, then you are listening not only to the words, but also to the feeling of what is being conveyed, to the whole of it, not part of it."

— **Jiddu Krishnamurti**

"The fear of death follows from the fear of life. A man who lives fully is prepared to die at any time."

— **Mark Twain**

"Do not dwell in the past; do not dream of the future; concentrate the mind on the present moment."

— **Gautama Buddha**

"If anyone tells you that a certain person speaks ill of you, do not make excuses about what is said of you, but answer, 'He was ignorant of my other faults, else he would not have mentioned these alone'."

— **Epictetus**

"For every minute you are angry you lose sixty seconds of happiness."

— **Ralph Waldo Emerson**

"Kinship with all creatures of the earth, sky, and water was a real and active principle. In the animal and bird world, there existed a brotherly feeling that kept us safe among them.... The animals had rights - the right of man's protection, the right to live, the right to multiply, the right to freedom, and the right to man's indebtedness.

This concept of life and its relations filled us with the joy and mystery of living; it gave us reverence for all life; it made a place for all things in the scheme of existence with equal importance to all."

— Chief Luther Standing Bear

"It is easy to hate and it is difficult to love. This is how the whole scheme of things works. All good things are difficult to achieve; and bad things are very easy to get."

— Confucius

"Your hand can seize today, but not tomorrow; and thoughts of your tomorrow are nothing but desire. Don't waste this breath."

— Omar Khayyam

"Never be in a hurry; do everything quietly and in a calm spirit. Do not lose your inner peace for anything whatsoever, even if your whole world seems upset."

— Saint Francis de Sales

"Every morning we are born again. What we do today is what matters most."

— Gautama Buddha

"Faith is taking the first step even when you don't see the whole staircase."

— Martin Luther King, Jr.

"Look at the sky. We are not alone. The whole universe is friendly to us and conspires only to give the best to those who dream and work."

— A. P. J. Abdul Kalam

"Everything that irritates us about others can lead us to an understanding of ourselves."

— C.G. Jung

"Man often becomes what he believes himself to be. If I keep on saying to myself that I cannot do a certain thing, it is possible that I may end by really becoming incapable of doing it. On the contrary, if I have the belief that I can do it, I shall surely acquire the capacity to do it even if I may not have it at the beginning."

— Mahatma Gandhi

"Be moderate in order to taste the joys of life in abundance."

— Epicurus

"Run my dear, from anything that may not strengthen your precious budding wings. Run like hell my dear, from anyone likely to put a sharp knife into the sacred, tender vision of your beautiful heart."

— Hafez (also known as Hafiz)

"Keep your face always towards the sunshine – and shadows will fall behind you."

— Walt Whitman

"For him in vain the envious seasons roll,
Who bears eternal summer in his soul."

— Oliver Wendell Holmes

"Until thought is linked with purpose there is no intelligent accomplishment. With the majority the bark of thought is allowed to "drift" upon the ocean of life. Aimlessness is a vice, and such drifting must not continue for him who would steer clear of catastrophe and destruction."

— James Allen

"There are two basic motivating forces: fear and love. When we are afraid, we pull back from life. When we are in love, we open to all that life has to offer with passion, excitement, and acceptance. We need to learn to love ourselves first, in all our glory and our imperfections. If we cannot love ourselves, we cannot fully open to our ability to love others or our potential to create. Evolution and all hopes for a better world rest in the fearlessness and open-hearted vision of people who embrace life."

— John Lennon

"Come forth into the light of things, let Nature be your teacher."

— William Wordsworth

"Happiness is when what you think, what you say, and what you do are in harmony."

— Mahatma Gandhi

"Dead yesterdays and unborn tomorrows, why fret about it, if today be sweet."

— Omar Khayyam

"To love. To be loved. To never forget your own insignificance. To never get used to the unspeakable violence and the vulgar disparity of life around you. To seek joy in the saddest places. To pursue beauty to its lair. To never simplify what is complicated or complicate what is simple. To respect strength, never power. Above all, to watch. To try and understand. To never look away. And never, never to forget."

— **Arundhati Roy, The Cost of Living**

"The ability to observe without evaluating is the highest form of intelligence."

— **Jiddu Krishnamurti**

"You wander from room to room
Hunting for the diamond necklace
That is already around your neck!"

— **Rumi**

"Calmness of mind is one of the beautiful jewels of wisdom. It is the result of long and patient effort in self-control. Its presence is an indication of ripened experience, and of a more than ordinary knowledge of the laws and operations of thought."

— **James Allen, As a Man Thinketh**

"Life is like riding a bicycle. To keep your balance, you must keep moving."

— **Albert Einstein**

"When I was 5 years old, my mother always told me that happiness was the key to life. When I went to school, they asked me what I wanted to be when I grew up. I wrote down 'happy'. They told me I didn't understand the assignment, and I told them they didn't understand life."

— **John Lennon**

"I have three precious things which I hold fast and prize. The first is gentleness; the second is frugality; the third is humility, which keeps me from putting myself before others. Be gentle and you can be bold; be frugal and you can be liberal; avoid putting yourself before others and you can become a leader among men."

— **Lao Tzu**

"I am fundamentally an optimist. Whether that comes from nature or nurture, I cannot say. Part of being optimistic is keeping one's head pointed toward the sun, one's feet moving forward. There were many dark moments when my faith in humanity was sorely tested, but I would not and could not give myself up to despair. That way lays defeat and death."

— **Nelson Mandela**

"Let your life lightly dance on the edges of time like dew on the tip of a leaf."

— **Rabindranath Tagore**

"You can only become truly accomplished at something you love. Don't make money your goal. Instead, pursue the things you love doing and then do them so well that people can't take their eyes off you."

— **Maya Angelou**

"If you are irritated by every rub, how will your mirror be polished?"

— **Rumi**

"I am in love with every church, and mosque, and temple, and any kind of shrine because I know it is there that people say the different names of the One God."

— **Hafez (also known as Hafiz)**

"Freedom and love go together. Love is not a reaction. If I love you because you love me, that is mere trade, a thing to be bought in the market; it is not love. To love is not to ask anything in return, not even to feel that you are giving something - and it is only such love that can know freedom."

— Jiddu Krishnamurti

"The more you know yourself, the more clarity there is. Self-knowledge has no end - you don't come to an achievement, you don't come to a conclusion. It is an endless river."

— Jiddu Krishnamurti

"Education is what survives when what has been learnt has been forgotten."

— B. F. Skinner

"The journey of a thousand miles begins with a single step."

— Lao Tzu

"There is only one way to happiness and that is to cease worrying about things which are beyond the power or our will."

— Epictetus

"Sorrow prepares you for joy. It violently sweeps everything out of your house, so that new joy can find space to enter. It shakes the yellow leaves from the bough of your heart, so that fresh, green leaves can grow in their place. It pulls up the rotten roots, so that new roots hidden beneath have room to grow. Whatever sorrow shakes from your heart, far better things will take their place."

— Rumi

"With begging and scrambling we find very little, but with being true to ourselves we find a great deal more."

— **Rabindranath Tagore**

"The secret of change is to focus all your energy,

Not on fighting the old, but on building the new."

— **Socrates**

"Stop acting so small. You are the universe in ecstatic motion."

— **Rumi**

"One is never afraid of the unknown; one is afraid of the known coming to an end…. You can only be afraid of what you think you know."

— **Jiddu Krishnamurti**

"I don't believe one grows older. I think that what happens early on in life is that at a certain age one stands still and stagnates."

— **T. S. Eliot**

"Every day we should hear at least one little song, read one good poem, see one exquisite picture, and, if possible, speak a few sensible words."

— **Johann Wolfgang von Goethe**

"After climbing a great hill, one only finds that there are many more hills to climb."

— **Nelson Mandela**

"I am not what happened to me; I am what I choose to become."

— C.G. Jung

"Don't cry because it's over, smile because it happened."

— Dr Seuss

"To surrender ego means to become constantly aware of that Reality that is within."

— Swami Rama Tirtha

"He who attends to his greater self becomes a great man, and he who attends to his smaller self becomes a small man."

— Mencius

"He who reigns within himself and rules his passions, desires and fears is more than a king."

— John Milton

"I have just three things to teach: simplicity, patience, compassion. These three are your greatest treasures."

— Lao Tzu

"People do not quit playing because they grow old; they grow old because they quit playing."

— Oliver Wendell Holmes

"How long are you going to wait before you demand the best for yourself and in no instance bypass the discriminations of reason? You have been given the principles that you ought to endorse, and you have endorsed them. What kind of teacher, then, are you still waiting for in order to refer your self-improvement to him? You are no longer a boy, but a full-grown man. If you are careless and lazy now and keep putting things off and always deferring the day after which you will attend to yourself, you will not notice that you are making no progress, but you will live and die as someone quite ordinary.

From now on, then, resolve to live as a grown-up who is making progress, and make whatever you think best a law that you never set aside. And whenever you encounter anything that is difficult or pleasurable, or highly or lowly regarded, remember that the contest is now: you are at the Olympic Games, you cannot wait any longer, and that your progress is wrecked or preserved by a single day and a single event. That is how Socrates fulfilled himself by attending to nothing except reason in everything he encountered. And you, although you are not yet a Socrates, should live as someone who at least wants to be a Socrates."

— Epictetus

"To understand the immeasurable, the mind must be extraordinarily quiet, still."

— Jiddu Krishnamurti

"I have walked that long road to freedom. I have tried not to falter; I have made missteps along the way. But I have discovered the secret that after climbing a great hill, one only finds that there are many more hills to climb. I have taken a moment here to rest, to steal a view of the glorious vista that surrounds me, to look back on the distance I have come. But I can only rest for a moment, for with freedom come responsibilities, and I dare not linger, for my long walk is not ended."

— Nelson Mandela

"Don't grieve. Anything you lose comes around in another form."

— Rumi

"To enjoy good health, to bring true happiness to one's family, to bring peace to all, one must first discipline and control one's own mind. If a man can control his mind, he can find the way to Enlightenment, and all wisdom and virtue will naturally come to him."

— Gautama Buddha

"Be not afraid of greatness: some are born great, some achieve greatness, and some have greatness thrust upon them."

— William Shakespeare

"If you begin to understand what you are without trying to change it, then what you are undergoes a transformation."

— Jiddu Krishnamurti

"A good head and good heart are always a formidable combination. But when you add to that a literate tongue or pen, then you have something very special."

— Nelson Mandela

"Choose a job you love, and you will never have to work a day in your life."

— Confucius

"You were born with wings; why prefer to crawl through life?"

— Rumi

"Your task is not to seek for love, but merely to seek and find all the barriers within yourself that you have built against it."

— A Course in Miracles

"Any person capable of angering you becomes your master; he can anger you only when you permit yourself to be disturbed by him."

— Epictetus

"Through pride we are ever deceiving ourselves. But deep down below the surface of the average conscience a still, small voice says to us, something is out of tune."

— C.G. Jung

"No one is born hating another person because of the colour of his skin, or his background, or his religion. People must learn to hate, and if they can learn to hate, they can be taught to love, for love comes more naturally to the human heart than its opposite."

— Nelson Mandela

"To transform the world, we must begin with ourselves, and what is important in beginning with ourselves is the intention. The intention must be to understand ourselves and not to leave it to others to transform themselves or to bring about a modified change through revolution, either of the left or of the right. It is important to understand that this is our responsibility, yours and mine...."

— Jiddu Krishnamurti

"Everybody is a genius. But if you judge a fish by its ability to climb a tree, it will live its whole life believing that it is stupid."

— Albert Einstein

"At times our own light goes out and is rekindled by a spark from another person. Each of us has cause to think with deep gratitude of those who have lighted the flame within us."

— Albert Schweitzer

"Ignore those who make you fearful and sad, who degrade you back towards disease and death."

— Rumi

"He who has a why to live can bear almost any how."

— Friedrich Nietzsche

"Each time I pass a shop I am amazed at the number of things man can do without."

— Socrates

"I am not a saint, unless you think of a saint as a sinner who keeps on trying."

— Nelson Mandela

"Other people's views and troubles can be contagious. Don't sabotage yourself by unwittingly adopting negative, unproductive attitudes through your associations with others."

— Epictetus

"There are only two ways to live your life. One is as though nothing is a miracle. The other is as though everything is a miracle."

— Albert Einstein

"Happiness is strange; it comes when you are not seeking it. When you are not making an effort to be happy, then unexpectedly, mysteriously, happiness is there, born of purity, of a loveliness of being."

— Jiddu Krishnamurti

"Care about what other people think and you will always be their prisoner."

— Lao Tzu

"Attach yourself to what is spiritually superior, regardless of what other people think or do. Hold to your true aspirations no matter what is going on around you."

— Epictetus

"As I walked out the door toward the gate that would lead to my freedom, I knew if I didn't leave my bitterness and hatred behind, I'd still be in prison."

— Nelson Mandela

"We reap what we sow. We are the makers of our own fate. None else has the blame, none has the praise."

— Swami Vivekananda

"The mind, once expanded to the dimensions of larger ideas, never returns to its original size."

— Oliver Wendell Holmes

"I long to accomplish a great and noble task, but it is my chief duty to accomplish small tasks as if they were great and noble."

— Helen Kelleumi

"Write it on your heart that every day is the best day in the year."

— Ralph Waldo Emerson

"An individual has not started living until he can rise above the narrow confines of his individualistic concerns to the broader concerns of all humanity."

— Martin Luther King Jr.

"He is a wise man who does not grieve for the things which he has not, but rejoices for those which he has."

— Epictetus

"It is only when the mind is free from the old that it meets everything anew, and in that there is joy."

— Jiddu Krishnamurti

"I speak to everyone in the same way, whether he is the garbage man or the president of the university."

— Albert Einstein

"Raise your words, not voice. It is rain that grows flowers, not thunder."

— Rumi

"As I have said, the first thing is to be honest with yourself. You can never have an impact on society if you have not changed yourself.... Great peacemakers are all people of integrity, of honesty, but humility."

— Nelson Mandela

"Teach this triple truth to all: a generous heart, kind speech, and a life of service and compassion are the things which renew humanity."

— Gautama Buddha

"Overcoming poverty is not a task of charity; it is an act of justice. Like slavery and apartheid, poverty is not natural. It is man-made and it can be overcome and eradicated by the actions of human beings. Sometimes it falls on a generation to be great. YOU can be that great generation. Let your greatness blossom."

— Nelson Mandela

"Caretake this moment. Immerse yourself in its particulars. Respond to this person, this challenge, this deed. Quit evasions. Stop giving yourself needless trouble. It is time to really live; to fully inhabit the situation you happen to be in now."

— Epictetus

"Try not to become a man of success. Rather become a man of value."

— Albert Einstein

"If we can really understand the problem, the answer will come out of it, because the answer is not separate from the problem."

— Jiddu Krishnamurti

"When one door of happiness closes, another opens, but often we look so long at the closed door that we do not see the one that has been opened for us."

— Helen Keller

"Thousands of candles can be lighted from a single candle, and the life of the candle will not be shortened. Happiness never decreases by being shared."

— Gautama Buddha

"If you are depressed, you are living in the past.
If you are anxious, you are living in the future.
If you are at peace, you are living in the present."

— Lao Tzu

"Holding on to anger is like grasping a hot coal with the intent of throwing it at someone else; you are the one who gets burnt."

— Gautama Buddha

"Don't put the key to your happiness in someone else's pocket."

— Swami Chinmayananda

"I want to sing like the birds sing, not worrying about who hears or what they think."

— Rumi

A leader... is like a shepherd. He stays behind the flock, letting the most nimble go out ahead, whereupon the others follow, not realising that all along they are being directed from behind."

— Nelson Mandela

"Work joyfully and peacefully, knowin that right thoughts and right efforts inevitably bring about right results."

— James Allen

"Great spirits have always encountered violent opposition from mediocre minds."

— Albert Einstein

"Not all of us can do great things. But we can do small things with great love."

— Mother Theresa

"Because one believes in oneself, one doesn't try to convince others. Because one is content with oneself, one doesn't need others' approval. Because one accepts oneself, the whole world accepts him or her."

— Lao Tzu

"If we could look into each other's hearts and understand the unique challenges each of us faces, I think we would treat each other much more gently, with more love, patience, tolerance and care."

— Marvin J. Ashton

"It is every man's obligation to put back into the world at least the equivalent of what he takes out of it."

— Albert Einstein

"There are as many nights as days, and the one is just as long as the other in the year's course. Even a happy life cannot be without a measure of darkness, and the word 'happy' would lose its meaning if it were not balanced by sadness."

— C.G. Jung

"There is no school equal to a decent home and no teacher equal to a virtuous parent."

— Mahatma Gandhi

"One of the things I learnt when I was negotiating was that, until I changed myself, I could not change others."

— Nelson Mandela

"Every beauty which is seen here by persons of perception resembles more than anything else that celestial source from which we all are come."

— **Michelangelo**

"When I chased after money, I never had enough. When I got my life on purpose and focussed on giving of myself and everything that arrived into my life, then I was prosperous."

— **Wayne Dyer**

"Let no one ever come to you without leaving better and happier. Be the living expression of God's kindness: kindness in your face, kindness in your eyes, kindness in your smile."

— **Mother Teresa**

"We suffer more often in imagination than in reality."

— **Seneca**

"To understand life is to understand ourselves, and that is both the beginning and the end of education."

— **Jiddu Krishnamurti**

"Yesterday is but a memory and tomorrow only a vision. But today well lived makes every yesterday a memory of happiness, and every tomorrow a vision of hope. Look well therefore to this day."

— **Kalidas**

"When you are content to be simply yourself and don't compare or compete, everyone will respect you."

— **Lao Tzu**

"Even the least work done for others awakens the power within; even thinking the least good of others gradually instils into the heart the strength of a lion."

— Swami Vivekananda

"A truly good book teaches me better than to read it. I must soon lay it down, and commence living on its hint. What I began by reading, I must finish by acting."

— Henry David Thoreau

"Use your health, even to the point of wearing it out. That is what it is for. Spend all you have before you die; do not outlive yourself."

— George Bernard Shaw

"I went to the woods because I wished to live deliberately, to front only the essential facts of life, and see if I could not learn what it had to teach, and not, when I came to die, discover that I had not lived. I did not wish to live what was not life, living is so dear; nor did I wish to practice resignation, unless it was quite necessary. I wanted to live deep and suck out all the marrow of life, to live so sturdily and Spartan-like as to put to rout all that was not life, to cut a broad swath and shave close, to drive life into a corner, and reduce it to its lowest terms."

— Henry David Thoreau

TWENTY

PERSONAL SUCCESS STORIES

I n this chapter, two individuals, R.K. Shetty and Laazarus Dias, who both attended my very first presentations in Bangalore, India in 1996, recount their stories of success. Kapil Mathur attended a workshop in Mumbai in 2002. The first and most recent story is on past MDRT MCC South Africa Chair, Kobus Kleyn. Each of these four stories can inspire readers to achieve more meaningful goals and aspirations in their lives.

KOBUS KLEYN'S STORY

Kobus Kleyn attended his first MDRT Annual Meeting in Philadelphia, USA, in June 2013. He sent a highly complementary email to MDRT Headquarters on his return, full of enthusiasm regarding his experience. I was informed of this and immediately contacted him and proposed his name for MDRT Membership Communications Committee, Area Chair Gauteng, from 1st September 2013. I'd never met Kobus before that but had a strong belief that he would make a great MDRT leader in South Africa based on his track record in our profession. I worked very closely with him. Not only did Kobus deliver what was expected of him, he exceeded all expectations. He devoted extraordinary efforts and time to promote awareness of MDRT, with an urgency, drive and enthusiasm that was delightful to witness. He performed so well in his role as Area Chair that I took the unprecedented step of nominating him to serve as Country Chair South Africa in only his 2nd year of membership. Kobus galvanized a powerful team around him and, under his inspiring leadership, MDRT membership in South Africa increased by a significant 23% over that year.

Below is Kobus Kleyn's story, in his own words

I joined the financial services profession on 1st August 2001 after 18 years working in the corporate world with some significant blue-chip organisations. I started as a mechanical engineer, successfully climbed the corporate ladder and my last job title was Divisional Managing Director. I decided to leave the corporate world and to follow my passion as an entrepreneur, where I could make a difference in people's lives while creating wealth and a balance in my own life. It took me a year to work through all entrepreneurial options by attending many small and medium enterprises and franchise expos until I came upon the Liberty Group offering on entrepreneurial advice partner's practices. It came with low entry barriers, and it met my 'Why' purpose and I could match it with my passion.

I built a successful practice until 2008 with advisors under this formula. I then decided to sell it to my partner, as it was again becoming a corporate, which I left to ensure a whole person lifestyle. I then followed my passion for serving my client base with a practice within the company I created. As a certified financial planner (CFP), I operated with a well-structured continuity team and admin support structure. I immediately decided to get more involved with MDRT, but initially, unofficially, until I joined officially in 2012. I also joined the Financial Planning Institute Southern Africa (FPI) and the Financial Intermediaries Association South Africa (FIA), enabling me to learn practice building techniques and gain more excellent knowledge about financial planning and our profession, both locally and internationally. Over time, I joined IISA, STEP, FISA, and The Ethics Institute to grow my value proposition and intellectual property.

I started following the MDRT best practices and operating systems in 2008, four years before becoming a full member. It gave me greater credibility, and I became an official member of MDRT in 2012 and was fortunate enough to attend the MDRT Annual Meeting and Experience meeting in my next year. I also qualified for MDRT Top of the Table (TOT) in my first year of membership. It was possible from the ideas and concepts I learned through my prior exposure to MDRT - from MDRT members, videos, magazines, MDRT's website and any other material I could lay my hands on. I have maintained my TOT status every year since and have become a proud MDRT Life Member in 2021.

I was blessed to have met long-standing MDRT stalwart, and Top of the Table member, Logan Naidu, in my first year with MDRT, which in itself was a life-changing event as he took a keen interest in me. Logan showed me pathways (especially after I read his profound book, Unleash Your Magic) within our profession, which I thought were not possible, or perhaps which I would not have contemplated if I did not meet him.

Logan is a seasoned MDRT mentor and not only believes in the MDRT Whole-Person Concept but lives it daily. Logan is an inspirational leader who has a passion for growing people through the concept of Self-Mastery. His published book "Unleash Your Magic" is one of the top 5 books (next to books like Long Walk to Freedom; Seven Habits of Highly Effective People, The Monk Who Sold His Ferrari and The Power of Now) I have read in my life, and that had a profound impact on my life. It has inspired me to pursue self-actualization further. Logan is a true gentleman and scholar, and I am proud to be associated with him and to have learned from him in my formative years with MDRT.

Logan took the bold step to nominate me as MDRT MCC Area Chair Gauteng South Africa, which threw me in the deep end within MDRT leadership, but I accepted the position and have never looked back. A much bigger surprise was in store for me the following year, when Logan nominated me for MDRT MCC Country Chair South Africa. It seemed like a significant challenge, especially when, after my term as Country Chair commenced, Logan was abruptly appointed as Divisional Vice President (DVP) of Member Communications in Division 2, which did not include South Africa. I lost my guiding beacon but was determined to make it through the term. I was fortunate that Logan introduced me to MDRT Past-President Brian Heckert, who I met over a breakfast during a conference, and with his guidance and inspiration, I took the position of MCC Country Chair South Africa on boldly, and have not looked back. Since then I have served on many committees, task forces and PGA up to the level of PGA Director.

One of the highlights in my short MDRT affiliation was when I was nominated and accepted the flag bearing duties for South Africa for the 2014 Annual Meeting in Toronto. MDRT has played a pivotal role in my transformation from managing a practice with advisors to focusing only on my practice and clients while building a sustainable hybrid virtual practice with continuity and succession in place.

However, very soon, I realized that there was much more to my passion. I fully embraced MDRT's Whole Person Philosophy and, with influence and guidance from Logan, and following his lead, this became a "Passion for my Profession" and movement, with over 25 000 financial professionals now connected to the movement on LinkedIn. More can be viewed on my LinkedIn profile and domain at www. kobuskleyn.com.

I decided to become a stakeholder within our financial services profession to give back for all that I benefitted from this profession and make a positive contribution as a dedicated volunteer for the benefit of fellow advisers and with many of my affiliations, associations and FSP's.

During the last couple of years, I decided to enhance my involvement with my affiliations, which now includes MDRT, FPI, FIA, FISA, SAIT, IISA, STEP, The Ethics Institute and Unashamedly Ethical.

I use every opportunity afforded to me through media, publications, presentations, workshops, speakers events and much more to give back to our profession to influence my fellow financial professional as newcomers to the profession. I do many pro-bono talks on behalf of organisations I support and external organisations. I have taken a leading role with key legislative processes, with some of my affiliations. Some of these include TCF, RDR, POPI, COFI etc. in South Africa.

Over time, I would hope to get more involved at higher levels of pro-bono work within our profession (possibly board positions with the FPI and FIA), enabling me to make a much more significant difference but keeping a balance of life. My primary vision and mission are to be part of a holistic team effort to elevate our industry into a profession with the same status as our counterparts in the legal and medical professions. It is a long-term dream and vision we should all work towards and, with the necessary commitment and teamwork, we can make it happen in the years ahead. I am also heavily involved with the mentorship of MDRT aspirants and across the profession, and I mentor on average, six people annually.

It was apparent to me in my early years, after selling the company I started in 2001, that I would not be able to get the balance in my life right between family time, work and my passion. I had to rely a lot on guidance from Logan Naidu and MDRT to sort this out sooner rather than later. Thankfully, I have moved forward significantly to achieve a balance between such diverse demands on my time. I can only thank

Logan, MDRT, and my affiliations, as well as my family, for their support - we are all now benefiting from a much better balance in life, including many overseas and local holidays and spending quality time together. Under my enhanced Virtual Practice, I have become a swallow/nomad adviser who can work anywhere and enjoy a whole lifestyle with my family globally.

My greatest reward and recognition would, however, be when I, together with all other essential stakeholders, witness our volunteer and pro-bono work leading to our profession being accorded the same status as other long-standing professions.

Kobus Kleyn Brief BIO:

Kobus Kleyn is a Certified Financial Planner at Kainos Wealth (Pty) Ltd. He obtained his Post Graduate Qualification in Financial Planning at the University of Free State (South Africa) and his MDP & AEP from UNISA (Southern Africa). He holds many other designations & qualifications.

He has and is serving on many past and current committees and task forces for the Million Dollar Round Table (MDRT), Financial Planning Institute of South Africa (FPI), Financial Intermediaries Association of Southern Africa (FIA) and Liberty Group over the years in the roles of Chairperson, Vice-Chair, Director and Assistant Director. He served as Area and then Country Chair for MDRT South Africa. Kobus also serves on NPO boards as Director and The South African Youth Project Organisation (SAYPO- Diepsloot) was his most recent NPO.

Kobus holds eleven consecutive Million Dollar Round Table Top of the Table recognitions and MDRT Life Membership status and is a well-recognized CFP in South Africa and globally, with a fully functional professional hybrid virtual Practice.

Kobus is affiliated with eight organisations, inclusive of the FPI (with the CFP designation); SAIT (South African Institute of Tax Practitioners, with the Tax Practitioner designation); FISA (Fiduciary Institute of Southern Africa); STEP (Society of Trust and Estate Practitioner, with a TEP designation); FIA (The Financial Intermediaries Association of Southern Africa); IISA (The Insurance Institute of South Africa); The Ethics Institute of South Africa; and Unashamedly Ethical.

He was the inaugural winner of the Financial Planning Institute's *"It Starts with Me"* award in 2015, received it again in 2016 and was awarded the *FPI Media Award in 2017.* He was awarded the MDRT Leadership Award (2014) and the President's Award (2019). He is a very active FPI, FIA and MDRT Pro-Bono Volunteer and an *MDRT Foundation Diamond Knight.* Kobus was awarded the Financial Planning Institute's prestigious Harry Brews Award in October 2021, which honours a remarkable individual for a lifetime of service to both the FPI and the financial planning profession in general.

Kobus has a **Passion** for the Financial Services Profession and works purposefully with like-minded stakeholders to help transform the financial industry into a fully-fledged profession. He accomplishes this through the power of social and print media, presentations, workshops, talks and with his involvement on committees.

Kobus has published over 200 articles on various media platforms and magazines. He has been a speaker at the Annual MDRT Convention, FPI Annual Convention, MDRT Greece Day, CARAIFA Annual Congress, BLISS and IFFA virtual events and on several other platforms locally and internationally. He is an inspirational speaker and takes the audience with him through energy and passion.

Kobus is rated in the top 1% on LinkedIn, with over 25 000 financial professionals connected to him globally. He uses LinkedIn as a movement to drive awareness to the financial services profession, the CFP Designations, Professionalism and the Power of Social Media.

He is a thought leader in many sectors, including the financial services profession, within the regulatory environments, on social media, personal branding, futuristic leadership, crypto & Blockchain technology, and other disruptive Fintech subjects.

Kobus is the author of the books *Passion for the Profession - Mastering the 9 P's to Professionalism,* **RDR** *- Mastering Key Elements to RDR and CryptoMania-Mastering the Crypto.* He will be launching his 4th book, *"Accelerate your Brand - Mastering your Brand,* in the near future.

Kobus has been invited to speak at the MDRT Global Conference to be held in Sydney, Australia on 28-31 August 2022.

> The world is your kaleidoscope, and the varying combinations of colours, which at evert succeeding moment it presents to you, are the exquisitely adjusted pictures of your ever-moving thoughts.
>
> — James Allen

R.K. SHETTY'S STORY

R.K. Shetty, B. Com, DFM, LUTCF (USA) attended my very first presentations in India in September 1996. He subsequently attended most of my other talks and workshops held in India over subsequent years. This is his story.

Below is R.K. Shetty's story, in his own words

The values I learnt from my parents formed the foundation for the both my professional and my personal achievements.

After graduation, I continued with my educational pursuits, holding multiple university degrees and industry designations.

My introduction to the life insurance field came unexpectedly. While running my income tax business, R K Shetty & Company, I was looking for new business opportunities to earn extra income, as my total monthly income was around $40. I joined the Life Insurance Corporation of India (LIC) in 1990 part-time. I immediately saw the benefits of additional income and began to love this profession where we can have such an impact on people's lives.

As a result of lack of knowledge, information and motivation during the first six years of my insurance career, I did the bare minimum required production and earned around $2, 000 per annum.

My life changed radically when I decided to attend a national level conference of the Life Insurance Round Table of India (LIRT) in Bangalore for the very first time in 1996 at a relatively high cost of

$500, which was as much as 25% of my annual income at that stage. That turned out to be a defining event in my life.

The major turning point happened when I heard Logan Naidu, who was a keynote speaker at that conference. Among other topics, he spoke about 'MDRT', 'MDRT Benefits', 'How to qualify for MDRT', 20 Point Plan and 'Creative Visualization'. He made a powerful case to all delegates to become MDRT members and to attend an MDRT Annual Meeting. The most appealing point to me was that, if I qualified, I would be invited to attend the members-only MDRT Annual Meeting in the USA. Visiting the USA was my long-standing dream, and I knew that, if I qualified, I would take an international flight for the very first time.

Logan further explained to us in practical detail how we could qualify for MDRT by using the '20 Point Plan' and 'Visualization' techniques, concepts that needed to be practiced daily. He convinced us that we could achieve any goal we set ourselves, provided we believe we can achieve it and take the necessary action.

Therefore, when all LIRT delegates heard Logan's presentations, and the way he motivated and inspired us, we were excited and enthusiastic, with everyone wanting to qualify for MDRT. I realised then that I could achieve significantly more than I ever imagined I could do. Logan made us all 'think big' and to be always conscious of our social responsibility by giving of ourselves unselfishly to help make a positive difference in people's lives.

I simply followed the process Logan recommended and worked hard to make sure I achieved my goals on a daily basis to qualify for MDRT. At that stage, I had just a small fraction of the MDRT qualification requirement, with a mere three months remaining to meet the requirement.

Well, the rest is history. Within three months of attending Logan's presentations in Bangalore, I rose from being an ordinary life insurance sales person in India to qualifying for the very first time for membership of the prestigious Million Dollar Round Table, The Premier Association of Financial Professionals globally, comprising around 2% of the world's top agents.

Logan was re-invited to do further presentations in Mumbai in 1997 and 2001, and I made sure I attended these, as well as a number of workshops he held subsequently.

From that LIRT convention onwards, there was no looking back. My life changed drastically when I attended my first MDRT Annual Meeting in Chicago, Illinois, in 1998. It was the unique philosophy of MDRT that drew me deeper into the organisation. After attending this meeting, I was not the same person anymore - my world had changed beyond recognition. Rather than be content with what I had already accomplished, I realised that I could set much larger goals for myself, including helping to expand the MDRT community in India. Since then, I have served in many leadership positions in MDRT, receiving numerous national and international awards, rewards and recognition.

R.K. Shetty Bio:

R.K. Shetty has gone on to become one of *the* most successful financial professionals in India and qualified for MDRT 26 years since 1997, including 18 consecutive times for Top of the Table. He assumed numerous senior positions within MDRT's leadership, being the first Indian to be appointed MCC Regional Chair and the first Indian to be appointed Divisional Vice President (DVP) in the 82-year history of MDRT, as well as Chair of the 2013 Hyderabad MDRT Experience Meeting Task Force. He was selected as a Special Session speaker at the MDRT Annual Meeting in Indianapolis in June 2009 and as a Main Platform speaker at the 'TOP OF THE TABLE' Annual Meeting held in Florida in 2010. In 2012, the Senate of the Open International University, Sri Lanka awarded him an Honorary Doctorate for his business management and humanitarian service.

RK also received a multitude of accolades and other awards from many organisations in India and engages in a number of socially responsible projects in India, as listed below:

- Served on MDRT's 2011 Leadership & Volunteer Development Committee.

- Main Platform Speaker and Focus Session Speaker for 13th APLIC Congress, held in 2011 in Singapore.

- 2010 recipient of "Karnataka Rajyotsava Award" from its Chief Minister, Honourable Shri B S Yediyurappa, for his achievements in Financial Services.

- Felicitated by Abhishek Bachchan & Aishwarya Rai Bachchan at the World Bunts Sports Festival, held in Mumbai in 2010.

- Numerous newspapers published articles on R.K. Shetty's life and achievements, including Indian Express, The Hindu, Financial Express, etc.

- A number of prominent TV Channels, such as CNBC, Zee TV, Sahara TV, invited him to participate in their prime time Talk Shows on the subject of Financial Management and Insurance.

- R.K is also a social activist and worked with physically handicapped people, distributed note books and uniform to poor & needy students, appointed a Kannada teacher in one of the Municipal School in Mumbai at his cost, provided educational financing for several students through Bunts Sangha, built a school in Kambihali, Chickmagalur, in Karnataka State, where he studied and helped in rebuilding a temple in this area.

He concludes: "When I look back on my life, I owe a great deal to Logan Naidu, who contributed so much to the course of my life. Being exposed to his presentations in 1996 was a life-changing experience for me. I attended most of his many presentations and workshops in India and he visited my offices on most of his many visits to India. I am asked to talk about my story extensively throughout India. As a result, Logan is well known among the insurance fraternity here, as my story of success cannot be complete without mentioning his name.

Therefore, I always have the highest respect and gratitude to Logan for the incredible impact he has had on my life."

— **Dr R.K. (Radhakrishna) Chetty B.COM, DFM, LUTCF (USA)**
Mumbai, India

"All that we are is the result of what we have thought: it is founded on our thoughts and made up of our thoughts. If a man speaks or acts with an evil thought, suffering follows him as the wheel follows the hoof of the beast that draws the wagon.... If a man speaks or acts with a good thought, happiness follows him like a shadow that never leaves him."

— **Gautama Buddha**

LAZARUS DIAS'S STORY

Lazarus Dias also attended the presentations at the Life Insurance Round Table of India (LIRT) in Bangalore, India in September 1996. This is his story.

Below is Laazarus Dias's story, in his own words

I met Logan Naidu at the LIRT Conference in Bangalore on 5 September 1996. I used to attend LIRT conventions even though I had never qualified for MDRT. I come from a very poor background and, based on my circumstances, I never thought that I had the kind of prospects who would take me to MDRT status. I used to get motivated by speakers, but never thought that specifically I could become an MDRT member. My own belief about myself and my circumstances prevented me from thinking about MDRT.

At that stage, I had no clue about my production figures towards MDRT qualification, as they were very low and I never checked them, as I was sure that I was too far from MDRT.

The presentation made by Logan on 'Creative Visualization' hit me like a bolt from the blue. I was shocked and stumped and it sounded almost unbelievable. I remember going to Logan and asking him if what he presented was really true. I could not believe it, but thought, why not try it out. After coming back to Mumbai, I adopted the three-step approach, to declare that I would qualify for MDRT, which I did to my wife, my manager and my coach. Secondly, I sat down every day for 15 minutes visualising that I had already qualified for MDRT and seeing in my mind's eye the journey to USA for the MDRT Annual Meeting, as Logan asked us to do. Thirdly, I applied for a passport, as I did not have one. Further, I sent a letter to all the LIRT attendees informing them that I was going to qualify for MDRT, that I had applied for a passport and that I was also preparing to attend the MDRT convention to be held in June 1997. I informed them to also apply for a passport and asked them to get ready to go to MDRT together with me.

Even though I had done the three things mentioned above, deep down in my heart, I still did not believe that I really could qualify for MDRT. There was no deep belief about the possibility of MDRT in my life.

After a few days, I was informed by LIRT Convention organiser, Mr PS Kochhar, that Logan was coming to Mumbai and he asked if I would take him for lunch. I immediately jumped at the idea. My wife, Sylvia, accompanied me to pick up Logan and his wife, Sussie, and we all went to the Jewel of India Restaurant for lunch. I was keen to have a heart to heart discussion with Logan and get further clarity on what he had shared at LIRT. Three hours went by and we did not know how the time had passed. I discussed with Logan in detail about creative visualization and the three steps that I had taken. He validated the same and encouraged me in my pursuit.

I entered the Jewel of India hotel with Logan with the mindset 'I CAN'T'. At the end of that meeting, I came out of the hotel with a firm belief: 'I CAN'. What a miracle! I then had absolutely no doubt that 'I AM POSSIBLE'.

I really did not know exactly what I did, but I practiced the concept of visualization on a daily basis and worked hard day in and day out. Lo and behold! I got the best two gifts of my life on 24 December 1996. My manager called to inform me that I had qualified for MDRT, and my wife delivered our second child, a baby girl whom we named Noella, but who was truly the MDRT baby.

I had appointed a Coach Atul Gore in 1996. I was the first agent in India to have a professional coach. Listening to Logan's presentations at the LIRT meeting, along with input and constant monitoring from the coach, helped me double my income year after year from 1996 till about 2001, by which time I had qualified for MDRT six times and my income had increased 10 times.

I attended the MDRT convention in Atlanta in June 1997 along with 20 other agents from Mumbai. This was a dream come true.

Since then, my life story became an instant hit in India and I started being called to many Life Insurance Corporation of India (LIC) branches to share my success story. I was invited as a speaker at the next LIRT convention in Mumbai in 1997 to share the secrets of my success. After the great impact he had in Bangalore, Logan was once again invited to do presentations at this convention.

After my speech at LIRT, many of my friends approached me to coach them in a professional way. I created the Laazarus Dias Education Akademy (LDEA) in Mumbai as I realised that, if I could reach the pinnacle of success from just listening to Logan's presentations and regular coaching, then many more could benefit in a similar way. Through the Laazarus Dias Education Akademy, I have trained more than 1,000 agents in Mumbai, addressed over a hundred thousand agents across India, published four books and I've been instrumental in making 200 agents qualify for MDRT membership.

PREDICTABLE SUCCESS WITH BALANCED LIFE

Lazarus Dias

Laazarus Dias Education Akademy

Website www.laazarusdias.in

www.skyllinc.com

> "To be what we are, and to become what we are
> capable of becoming, is the only end in life."
>
> — **Robert Louis Stevenson**

KAPIL MATHUR'S STORY, IN HIS OWN WORDS

It was the Indian summer of 2002, in the month of July. I had just made a career switch from British Petroleum after a successful stint of 5 years. I joined ICICI Prudential to head up a successful team of 17 Unit Managers managing teams comprising 250 tied agents. In fact, I had been selectively head hunted for my Sales & Distribution skills. In recruiting talent from outside, the organization positioned my appointment as a major boost to their growth plans. Expectations from me were high.

My boss was a young, dynamic, hard task master, Anup Rau, now CEO of Reliance Life Insurance. He was a huge support and made me a core part of his growth plans. However, within a matter of days the honeymoon period was over and expectations from me were benchmarked.

I quickly realized I had made an error of judgment by changing my industry from lubricants to Insurance, one at which I had no experience or skill set. To grapple with the new challenges and expectations, I did what I thought I should. I read the product features and made every effort to grapple with the challenges I faced, without much success. Something was missing and I found myself sliding backwards. Some members of my team, who had been overlooked while I was installed as their line manager, spared no effort to make me look inexperienced and out of place in this business. They approached the Regional Head and complained at his lack of judgment in installing me as their leader. To his credit, he dismissed their complaints and put his full weight behind me. In spite of this, I felt it was now a matter of time before I licked my wounds, accepted my mistake and moved on to another industry. After all, mistakes can be made. But, I knew deep down, I had not given this my very best. I was gripped with moments of anger, guilt and helplessness and deeply regretted making this aggressive career change.

One day, while glancing through the local Mumbai papers, I saw a small advertisement "UNLEASH YOUR MAGIC - Double your Productivity," by Logan Naidu. It was the first seminar dedicated to insurance that I came across, so I decided to attend. When you have nothing left to lose, you then have everything to gain. It was a 9:00 am - 5:00 pm session, and I was given the day off to attend the program at my own expense.

I went to the seminar, eager to see what this man from South Africa had to offer and hear about this magic formula to double my business. The program started with Logan taking the stage with African music playing in the background and all the razzmatazz. I sat there with an open mind to absorb everything. The 300 attendees were all tied agents from various major insurance companies, including Life Insurance Corporation of India (LIC), and MDRT aspirants.

More than the words, I connected to Logan's sheer passion and joy of being in this business. I marvelled at the ease of his delivery and realized this was a business from the 'heart to the heart' and everything else was mere paperwork. I completely immersed myself in his daylong session, making copious notes and connected with the vibe of visualizing my goals, believing in what I'm doing, implementing the required strategies and achieving success. After the session, as I walked back from the hotel to our office, I realized I had got my blueprint for success and felt supremely confident with the knowledge and actionable ideas to continue my journey in this business.

In my next meeting at ICICI Prudential, I declared to my boss that I was ready to turbo-charge the business but I needed a free hand to work it my way. In the days ahead, I began furiously implementing my learnings. Small successes bring reassurance and the upward spiral began to unfold. I began calling team meetings of groups of 30-odd tied agents and they connected with me, in the same way I connected to Logan, and the vast majority saw a manager who cared. I found myself leading client meetings and closing out large cases with Bollywood celebrities and business owners. These closures made money for the tied agents and they were grateful for my support and put their weight behind me. The word spread in the organization and I found myself being requested on all large-ticket cases.

For the first time, I was in love with this rare and noble profession. I was given larger roles and began climbing the corporate ladder. I connected with my 300 plus tied agents, who were managed by Unit Managers who began to accept my leadership.

In 2004, I visited Dubai and decided to move here, joining Standard Chartered Bank in Wealth Management. In a few years, I spearheaded the insurance selling for the bank and grew to Head of Sales for the UAE business.

I believed the real action is in financial planning and direct sales, not managing teams to deliver the sales numbers. There is nothing more satisfying than putting together a financial solution for a family and I built clients on the sheer passion and joy of forging relationships.

My clients saw a different person from a conventional life insurance sales person out to sell and move on. I cared and I loved them for giving me their trust. My business grew on the introductions my clients gave to their family and friends.

However, my heart yearned to be directly in the front of the customer. I loved being face to face with the client, listening to their aspirations and fears for their lives and family. In 2011, I made the decision to follow my heart and joined Holborn Assets, a leading firm in the business of financial planning in the UAE.

I qualified for the prestigious MDRT in the very first year, and every year since then. However, I did not attend the MDRT Annual Meeting till the 4th year. In June 2014 I went to my first MDRT meeting. On the very first day, I bumped into a charming lady, Yolie Aleman-Rodriguez, from Arizona, USA. We got chatting and I briefly narrated to her about myself and how I got into the business and mentioned how this all began with one seminar with Logan Naidu. She told me she too was mentored by Logan. Two people from two sides of the globe being touched by the same man. This was indeed a surreal experience and as we were chatting away she asked me to turn around, and who do I see, but the man himself, Logan Naidu.

I got the warmest hug of my life and it was a moment in time when life comes full circle. Logan and I went to the Starbucks next to the convention Centre and as I began telling him about my life journey, a calm descended on me. It was surreal to be sitting with someone who changed the path of your life and does not even know that, had it not been for that seminar in Mumbai 12 years earlier, I would not even be in this great industry.

I thank the Lord for keeping watch over me during my darkest hours, when even I was going to give up on me. Attending Logan's Mumbai Seminar made all the difference. It all started with seeing the simple small advertisement in the Mumbai local paper, "UNLEASH YOUR MAGIC - Double your Productivity" with Logan Naidu.

In the years since that day, I have attended every seminar on personal development and consider myself a lifelong learner.

Life has not been good, it has been exhilarating and I know I have a purpose in my life of giving back to this glorious business of life insurance. Thank you, Logan for the impact you had on my life.

Kapil Mathur, MBA, CISI (UK)
Senior Associate | Holborn Assets Ltd.
Dubai
United Arab Emirates

> "You were born with potential.
> You were born with goodness and trust.
> You were born with ideals and dreams.
> You were born with greatness.
> You were born with wings.
> You are not meant for crawling, so don't.
> You have wings.
> Learn to use them and fly."

- Rumi

> "True happiness is to enjoy the present, without anxious dependence upon the future, not to amuse ourselves with either hopes or fears but to rest satisfied with what we have, which is sufficient, for he that is so wants nothing. The greatest blessings of mankind are within us and within our reach. A wise man is content with his lot, whatever it may be, without wishing for what he has not."

— Seneca

CONCLUSION

"Everyone thinks of changing the world, but no one thinks of changing himself."

— Socrates

Thank you for purchasing and reading this book. Hopefully, you can benefit from some of the concepts shared and apply these in your business and your personal life.

Much information, ideas and concepts have been shared. This is the knowledge gained, over many decades, from MDRT experiences as well as exposure to the philosophy of Vedanta. This information or knowledge needs to be reflected upon by you, for a period of time. If this reflection is done conscientiously, and you assimilate and absorb the knowledge, it will bring about a transformation in you and you will gain wisdom. No one can give you wisdom, nor can the contents of this book do so. In fact, nobody outside yourself can give you wisdom. It is the knowledge diligently reflected upon that converts into wisdom. When you gain wisdom in an idea or concept, you live it.

In the final analysis, it is important to note that all the presentations and conferences we attend, all the speakers we listen to, and all the books we read will have no meaning and significance if we do not make the fundamental decision to implement at least one or two ideas learnt. I appeal to every reader to pick up just one idea or concept from this book and apply it in your life. Any new idea takes some time getting used to, but persevere and practice it every day for at least 30 days until it becomes a habit. You will undoubtedly experience the benefits that will accrue.

In closing, you may want to adopt this personal challenge which is guaranteed to ensure that you will enjoy a richer, happier, healthier and more productive life.

> "We should promise ourselves to be so strong that nothing could disturb our peace of mind. We should talk health, happiness and prosperity to every person we meet. We should make all of our friends and family and all those whose lives we touch feel that they've got something special and important in them. We should look at the bright side of everything and make our optimism come true. We should think only the best, work only for the best, and expect only the best. We should be just as enthusiastic about the success of others as we are about our own. We should forget the mistakes of our past, and press on to the greater achievements of the future. We should wear a cheerful face at all times and give every living creature we meet a smile. We should give so much time to the improvement of ourselves that we have no time to criticize others. We should be too large for worry, too noble for anger, too strong for fear and too happy to permit the presence of trouble."
>
> **— From the Optimist Creed, slightly adapted.**

You have the intelligence, genius, power and magic inside you. You can achieve significantly more than you imagine you are capable of. Let the light within you shine so brightly that the whole world can see you in all your glory.

UNLEASH YOUR MAGIC!

"Take up one idea. Make that one idea your life - think of it, dream of it, live on that idea. Let the brain, muscles, nerves, every part of your body, be full of that idea, and just leave every other idea alone. This is the way to success."

— **Swami Vivekananda**

"Great men are they who see that spiritual is stronger than any material force, that thoughts rule the world."

— **Ralph Waldo Emerson**

"The sole meaning of life is to serve humanity."

— **Leo Tolstoy**

"Live as if you were to die tomorrow. Learn as if you were to live forever."

— **Mahatma Gandhi**

"Why are you so enchanted by this world
When a mine of gold lies within you?
Open your eyes and come.
Return to the root of the root of your own Soul.
Set your life on fire.
Seek those who fan your flames"

— **Rumi**

ABOUT THE AUTHOR

Logan ventured into the financial services industry almost by default. Prior to discussing that, he thought it was important to know where he came from and some of the important influences on his life.

The starting point is 25 Buffalo Road, Dindigul, Tamil Nadu, India - home address of his maternal great-grandfather, Kisten Pillay, over 170 years ago in the 1850's. He had a tobacco business, which was characteristic of that part of the sub-continent. His youngest son Kumarasamy (popularly known as KK Pillay), who was born on 25 December 1867, was fired up with the spirit of adventure. He found an opportunity to realize his ambition when he was told that the Natal Colony in South Africa (now Kwazulu Natal) was a land of promise and that he should go there.

"All our dreams can come true, if we have the courage to pursue them."

— Walt Disney

The first few Indians in South Africa were imported by the Dutch East India Company, during the Dutch colonial era, as slaves, in 1684. The majority, however were brought here from 1860 by the British Government as indentured labourers[1] to work on the sugar cane plantations. Around 152,184 Indians arrived over a period of 5 decades. By the 1880's, some Indians began to open shops or trade as hawkers.

Indians faced discrimination to varying degrees in all the parts of South Africa – Natal, Cape Colony, Transvaal and Orange Free State. They were forced to carry passes in 1888 and banned from working in the mining industry. They were prohibited from living in the Orange Free State.

Persons of colour were not even permitted to walk on sidewalks in the Transvaal. The Indians lived in atrocious conditions, worked in the fields from morning till evening, their wages were low and sometimes they were not paid. Once the worker had completed his period of indenture he could return home or continue to find employment here. As many could not afford to go back to India, they chose to remain in Natal. Others chose to remain as they saw opportunities to prosper here. Some re-indentured and some leased or bought small plots of land which they cultivated. They lived frugally and saved to ensure their children were educated. As there were no schools or religious institutions, they collected funds and built their own facilities.

A key factor that helped forge a common South African "Indian" identity was the political struggles waged against harsh discriminatory

---

1   The **Indian indenture** system was a system of indentured servitude, by which more than one million Indians were transported to labour in European colonies, as a substitute for slave labour, following the abolition of the slave trade in the early 19th century.
Source: https://en.wikipedia.org/wiki/Indian_indenture_system

laws enacted against Indians and the other Black oppressed groups in the country. As a consequence, the Indian community established a number of political formations, the most prominent being the Natal Indian Congress (NIC) established by Mahatma Gandhi in 1894, and the Transvaal and Cape Indian Congresses in the early part of the 20th century. From 1945, the NIC worked alongside other liberation organizations like the African National Congress (ANC).

This demonstrates the determination and perseverance of the early Indians, who overcame the tremendous hardships they faced. Many of them made South Africa their permanent home, fully integrating into every aspect of our beautiful country. These enterprising pioneers are owed a great debt of gratitude for the great sacrifices they endured to create a better future for succeeding generations.

> "He who would accomplish little need sacrifice little; he who would achieve much must sacrifice much. He who would attain highly must sacrifice greatly."
>
> — James Allen

At the age of seventeen Logan's grandfather Kumarasamy signed on to be an indentured labourer. He boarded the ship "Laurel", along with 302 of his compatriots and departed from Madras (now Chennai) on 22 August 1884. After a voyage across the seas lasting a staggering thirty-six days, the Laurel arrived in Port Natal (now Durban) on 27 September 1884. Kumarasamy had received a good education in English and Tamil in India and upon arrival in Durban, he was employed as a messenger by the renowned estate agent, R. Acutt & Sons. After completing his contractual period of three years, he married Logan's grandmother, Amrootham. She was born in Madras in 1884 and came to South Africa at the age of four with her parents.

Due to his foresight and enterprising nature, KK Pillay declined an opportunity to renew his contract for a further term with the estate agent and instead opted to go to Johannesburg with his family. There he found employment in a large hotel. It was the time of the Anglo-Boer War and the hotel was used as a billet. As part of his duties, he served Paul Kruger, a frequent visitor to the hotel, who took a personal liking to him. Kruger was President of South Africa from 1883-1890. The hotel was subsequently named after him. When the war ended, KK Pillay gave up his hotel employment and it is reported that Paul Kruger presented him with a valuable parting gift.

"Set your life on fire. Seek those who fan your flames."

— Rumi

While in Johannesburg, his grandfather learnt to read and speak Afrikaans fluently and amassed a little wealth by saving gold Kruger sovereigns. The name KK Pillay and the suburb of Greenwood Park in Durban North are synonymous. On his return to Durban, he bought 14 acres of land there, extending from Park Station Road to Workington Road, which became famous as the "Pillay Mile" and still bears hallmarks of KK Pillay. Kumarasamy and Amrootham had thirteen children - seven daughters and six sons, each of whom eventually inherited portions of the Greenwood Park land. Logan's late mother, their youngest daughter Punjarathnam (1917-1983), inherited an acre of land in Workington Road, Greenwood Park. It was just bush at that time and they built on it much later, as explained below. Unfortunately,

Logan did not have the privilege of meeting any of his grandparents as they all passed away long before he was born.

KK Pillay sold part of the land he bought and used the remainder for growing fruit, coconut and vegetables. Logan's grandmother was an enthusiastic gardener and used the money she had saved from gardening to donate towards the building of a shrine in Umgeni Road, Durban. She was also an amazing hostess who had occasion to entertain visiting Agents-General from India and the renowned political activist and poet **Sarojini Naidu**[2].

An astute businessman and philanthropist, KK Pillay's considerable business acumen and initiative resulted in the establishment of a general dealer store, tea-room, drapery and butchery in Briardene in 1901. He was always concerned with the welfare of the community. He played an active role in establishing an English school in Greenwood Park and ensured that Tamil was taught here in the afternoons. Besides personally contributing, he raised funds from the public for the building of a temple in his home district, which still stands.

He served as Trustee of numerous organisations and contributed liberally to many educational, cultural, religious and charitable institutions. Education and health were foremost in his mind and he made a substantial contribution to the Sastri College Building Fund when the need for secondary education became important. He stressed the need of education as a passport to the world. Strinivasa Sastri was the first Agent-General for the Government of India in South

---

2   Sarojini Naidu was a proponent of civil rights, women's emancipation and anti-imperialistic ideas and an important figure in India's struggle for independence from colonial rule. She was appointed as the President of the Indian National Congress in 1925 and later became the Governor of the United Provinces in 1947, becoming the first woman to hold the office of Governor in the Dominium of India.

Africa and his services to South Africans were significant. He was the founder of the prestigious Sastri College, which stands as a monument to the dedication of the early pioneers in education. Sastri became a close associate of his grandfather and paid the family many visits.

KK Pillay also contributed towards the development of McCords Zulu Hospital in Durban. His association with the hospital went back many years to the time of Doctor Allen Taylor, the superintendent of the hospital, who was also the doctor of the Pillay family. On one of his visits to the family home in Greenwood Park, Dr. Taylor encouraged his youngest son to study medicine, which he did. Thus his mother's youngest brother became a doctor and subsequently so did many of KK Pillay's grandchildren and great-grandchildren.

The Pillays were also pioneers in sport and they formed a sports club in 1927. Even sporting bodies benefitted from KK Pillay's goodwill as he donated a piece of land in Greenwood Park for the erection of tennis courts. He invited Sir Kurma Reddi, Agent-General of India to open the tennis courts and a grand tea party was held to celebrate this historic event. It was indeed a progressive step in the lives of the women of Greenwood Park, as they were the first women to play tennis.

Logan's grandfather was a staunch supporter of the **Passive Resistance Campaign**[3] and marched into the Transvaal in 2013 under

---

3   The passive resistance campaigns led by MK Gandhi in South Africa had huge consequences not only for the history of the country but also for world history in general. Gandhi's campaigns forged a new form of struggle against oppression that became a model for political and ethical struggles in other parts of the world – especially in India's struggle for independence, South Africa's anti-apartheid movement and the United States civil rights campaign of the 1960s. Gandhi's 21 years in South Africa were formative in his mission to lead India's freedom struggle. Martin Luther King Jr. drew heavily on the Gandhian principle of nonviolence in his own civil rights activism, writing that *"while the Montgomery boycott was going on, India's Gandhi was the guiding light of our technique of nonviolent social change."* Nelson Mandela considered Gandhi as one of his teachers and said that he called for non-violent protest for as long as it was effective. Mandela led a peaceful campaign after release from prison with emphasis on reconciliation and a unique approach of forgiving the enemy. In the 1980's, the UDF[4] also took up the principle of non-violent resistance in South Africa, with many of its leaders specifically citing Gandhi as an influence.

the leadership of Mahatma Gandhi. He also served as an Executive Member of the Natal Indian Congress.

> "A small body of determined spirits fired by an unquenchable faith in their mission can alter the course of history."
>
> — Mohandas K. Gandhi

Logan's earliest recollections are of living in a rented outbuilding in Greenwood Park, being one of five children. They subsequently moved into their own two-bedroom wood and iron house on the plot of land his mother inherited from her father. That's where Logan can remember spending most of his younger life. They had no electricity, no hot water and no sewerage.

Logan's mum Punjarathnam Naidu (daughter of KK Pillay), married his dad, Ramsamy (Ram) Naidu (1913-1985), who also came from a pioneering family in Greenwood Park (unfortunately, there are no documents detailing his paternal grandfather's arrival in South Africa). Both his mum and dad were very caring, compassionate human beings who were humble, devoted and loving parents.

Although he had little formal education, Logan's Dad read widely. He was fluent in reading and writing, and he spoke three languages – Tamil, Telegu and English. He could also converse in basic Zulu. He had a large collection of books and encouraged his children to read from an early age. His mother was more the disciplinarian in the family, while simultaneously being fun-loving and an entertainer and cook *par excellence*. While they were schooling, it was not unusual for her to come to the soccer ground, or anywhere else he and his brothers happened to be after a length of time, to drag them home.

They continued living in the wood and iron house until Logan was 20 years old. As they had no electricity, he completed all his school studies, right up to Matric, by candlelight. His eldest brother Jaya had to leave school early so he could work to supplement the family's income. Although they grew up in relatively poor conditions, they had a great sense of belonging and their parents always taught them to do the right thing.

> "The best portion of a good man's life is his little, nameless, unremembered acts of kindness and of love."
>
> **— William Wordsworth**

Due to his family's finances, and as his elder two brothers Jaya and Kribbs had done, Logan started work immediately after high school. His first job was as a school school secretary at the Anjuman Islam School in Durban. During his stay there, the principal, M.S. Ismail, had a stroke and took quite ill. Although Logan wasn't even 20 years old at the time, he felt a great deal of compassion – he cared for him, he 'looked out' for him, and held his hand when he needed to walk.

MS Ismail was a kind and generous man and, even though he came to rely on Logan to a very large extent, he unselfishly motivated, and strongly supported, his promotion to the education department's head office, which happened soon thereafter. When Logan left the school in 1972, Mr Ismail broke down and cried and, in his own handwriting, which was adversely affected by his stroke, he wrote the following on a piece of paper and signed it:

"Goodbye, Mr Naidu.

I'll be watching your progress very closely. May you rise to the highest in your department is my humble prayer. May God bless you."

Sincerely

MS Ismail

Mr Ismail has passed on, but that note has been a great source of inspiration to Logan.

It was only when Logan was 20 that his family were able to build their own brick and tile house with electricity, hot water and sewerage for the princely sum of R 15, 000 (at that time, the Rand was equal in value to the US Dollar).

The story of his grandfather and his parents comprises the foundation of Logan's life. He doesn't want to forget where he came from and the immense sacrifices his forebears made to ensure that the generations that followed them can live in freedom. Logan is currently the only one of his direct descendants to come full circle – returning to the source, as it were. He relocated from South Africa to Pune, India in March 2016, enrolling at the end of the same month for the three-year residential course in Vedanta Philosophy at the Vedanta Academy, commencing with live lectures by Swami Parthasarathy on his newly-released book "Thesis on God". It has been a fascinating, transformative experience studying and imbibing this ancient knowledge contained in the Bhagavad Gita, Upanishads, and other such literature. The profound knowledge gained and life lessons learned are covered in chapters 16 and 17.

Logan worked at the offices of the Department of Indian Affairs for the next two years. This was one of the many 'separate' government departments at the height of the Apartheid regime in South Africa.

In 1974, Logan joined a large multinational oil company, Mobil, as a process technician. This new job involved shift work of six days on and two days off, with shift times being 8:00 am to 4:00 pm, 4:00 pm to midnight, and midnight to 8:00 am, the last shift being known as the graveyard shift.

While at Mobil, Logan helped to form an alternative non-racial social club, as the one that existed was reserved for whites only. He was elected its first secretary and, within two years, was elected chairman. The club organised a multitude of functions for members and their families. Logan loves children and the highlight of the calendar year was the Christmas party for the members' children. Specially purchased gifts, which he was personally involved in selecting, were handed to the kids by 'Father Christmas', who would arrive in style in the refinery's fire engine. The pure delight on the faces of the children made all their efforts worthwhile.

> "Happiness, not in another place but this place.
> Not for another hour but this hour."
>
> — **Walt Whitman**

Six months after joining Mobil – and while still employed there full-time – Logan joined the financial services industry and was given a contract with what was then African Eagle Life. For the next six years – 1974 to 1980 – he held down the two jobs – shift work at Mobil and selling life insurance – many times going straight into a Monday morning African Eagle team meeting directly after a midnight to 8:00 am shift.

F.M. Paul (Fred), who headed the Durban East team, was a manager *par excellence* and a leader of the highest calibre, who intuitively knew how to get the best out of the team. As a result, they were *the* most successful team in the country. The team comprised many highly politically conscious individuals, including Logan, who were actively involved in anti-apartheid activities. They often spent half of the weekly team meetings talking politics – remember this was in the 1980's, with apartheid at its peak, long before the advent of democracy in South Africa. Fred Paul was unbelievably tolerant and allowed such discussions to go on uninterrupted. They also held a get-together of newly arrived political exiles and formerly banned senior anti-apartheid leaders to their offices soon after political organizations in South Africa were unbanned on February 2, 1990. Logan was MC for that event and a number of those who attended were subsequently appointed as Ministers in President Nelson Mandela's first Cabinet, after the first-ever democratic elections in South Africa on that historic day, April 27, 1994.

Logan quit Mobil and joined the financial services industry full-time in May 1980, two months after he married Sussie.

Very early on in his career, he realised that setting goals was vitally important.

The three main goals he set in his first year full-time - 1981 - were to qualify for:

1. Membership of the prestigious Million Dollar Round Table.
2. His company's National Sales Convention (less than 10% of agents qualify for this).
3. LIMRA's International Quality Award (measured over two years).

He made his company's sales convention in 1981 and, based on his 1981 production, qualified as a provisional applicant for the 1982 MDRT (at that time, one could not qualify as a full MDRT member the first year, as one can currently, but only in one's second year of qualification). This meant more to him than any other award up to that stage and thus began his passion for MDRT. He qualified for the International Quality Award the following year as one needed to have records for a minimum of two years. He had just proven to himself the importance of setting goals.

Having completed all the company's training courses, he was looking for a challenge. An opportunity presented itself in 1981 when the Institute of Life and Pension Advisers (ILPA) was formed. The institute's main aim was to raise the level of professionalism in the industry and to set exams for a professional qualification that would be equivalent to the American CLU and ChFC - it was subsequently converted to the CERTIFIED FINANCIAL PLANNER (CFP®) professional designation. Logan was determined from the outset to sit for the first ever ILPA exams to be held in April 1982. He was too naive to listen to the views of many 'well-informed' people who stated that the first exams were going to be impossible to pass, that it was mainly for companies' 'legal advisors' and other 'experts' in our business. To make things more difficult, there were no study guides and no lectures - only a set of recommended books. In the words of Tommy Lasorda:

"The difference between the impossible and the possible lies in a person's determination."

Logan was determined to pass. As it happened, he passed all four subjects at the first sitting and was subsequently admitted as a Fellow of ILPA (FILPA) at the glittering Inaugural Banquet held at the Carlton Hotel, Johannesburg, on 3 September 1982.

Acquiring the FILPA qualification boosted his confidence, especially considering the pass rate was only about 15% and he was the only person from his company Southern Life to achieve this.

At the end of that same year – 1982, Logan enrolled to commence a Bachelor of Commerce degree by correspondence through the University of South Africa (UNISA). He started with two subjects. He happened to get 92% for Economics and UNISA waived fees for 2 subjects the following year, so he paid for another 2 subjects and did 4 subjects in 1983. He completed the 12 subjects - comprising 22 papers in four years, majoring in Economics and Business Economics.

"What you get by achieving your goals is not as important as what you become by achieving your goals."

— Henry David Thoreau

His graduation ceremony in 1987 was one of mixed emotions. It was indeed a very happy occasion, but one that was also very sad. He is grateful for the sacrifice made by Sussie and his two very young daughters at that time, Sarisha and Linestha. Sarisha was barely a few months old when he started studying towards FILPA and then the B. Com degree, and Linestha was born a few years later. Sussie was a pillar of strength and played an invaluable role both at home and in his insurance career and endured his political involvement in the anti-Apartheid struggle.

Logan was politically conscious from a very young age and played an active role in community organizations. He was chair of one of the founding affiliates of the **United Democratic Front**[4] - the Greenwood Park Ratepayers Association - and that also took up a fair portion of his time. He took over the position of Chairman from leading anti-apartheid activist and stalwart, Thumba Pillay, who Nelson Mandela appointed as a Judge in 1998.

4 The **United Democratic Front (UDF)** was one of the most important anti-Apartheid organisations of the 1980's. The non-racial coalition of about 400 civic, church, students, workers and other organisations (national, regional and local) was formed in 1983 and, considering the fact that the African National Congress (ANC) was banned at that stage, rapidly became *the* most prominent organisation internally in the anti-Apartheid struggle. The UDF's goal was to establish a "non-racial, united South Africa in which segregation is abolished and in which society is freed from institutional and systematic racism." Its rallying slogan, 'UDF Unites, Apartheid Divides', reflected the front's broad support (about three million members).

Logan meeting 'the father of the South African Nation' Nelson Mandela at a banquet in Madiba's honour in Durban before he became President

As an anti-apartheid activist in the late 1970's and throughout the 1980's and 90's, Logan publically called for the abolition of apartheid and full voting rights for all the people of South Africa in meetings and published letters in all major newspapers. He became a member of the African National Congress (ANC) as soon as it was unbanned on 2nd February 1990, culminating in our first democratic elections in 1994 with Nelson Mandela being elected president of a free South Africa. He had the great pleasure and privilege of briefly meeting Nelson Mandela on three occasions.

The real sadness, however, was that both his parents died within the four years that it took to complete his B. Com degree. His mom died on 13 July 1983, and dad on 17 November 1985. Those were really big blows in his life. He thought how very proud they would have been to see their son graduate with a degree. This would have been a first in their family at that stage. He remains eternally grateful for the life lessons they imparted to him and his siblings. They instilled in them the correct values in life, taught them about principles, honesty, truth, integrity, about caring, compassion, loving, humility, that nobody was superior to us, and so much more.

His mother was a fun-loving person and their house - whether it was the wood and iron or the brick house - was always a hub of liveliness, fun and laughter.

"Sometimes the poorest man leaves his children the richest inheritance."

— **Ruth E. Renkel**

"All power is within you. You can do anything and everything. Believe in that. Do not believe that you are weak. Stand up and express the divinity within you."

— **Swami Vivekananda**

Logan played a very active role in the Million Dollar Round Table (MDRT), The Premier Association of Financial Professionals, from the time he became a member in the 1980's. He served in various capacities in the Program General Arrangements Committees at Annual Meetings, numerous MDRT Committees, as Chair of the Pilot Sales Ideas Committee South Africa in 1998, Membership Communications Committees (MCC), as MCC Chair South Africa, MCC Zone Chair Middle East & & Africa, MDRT Ambassador, MDRT Speaker and as the 2014 - 2015 Divisional Vice-President (DVP) of Member Communications of MDRT, which included serving on MDRT's Management Council, the organisation's governing body.

As DVP, Logan oversaw three committees representing different regions around the world, including Japan, Korea, China, Hong Kong, Macau, Taiwan, South Asia (incl. India and Sri Lanka) and South-East Asia (incl. Philippines, Singapore, Indonesia, Malaysia, Thailand and Vietnam). The committee members are responsible for monitoring industry activities and involvement in their respective regions, as well as promoting MDRT to members and prospective members worldwide. They also act as a communication link between MDRT leadership and membership at large. Logan also served on MDRT Foundation's International Task Force and as Chair of the 2016 MDRT Foundation Global Engagement Committee.

Logan is a 41-year member of the Million Dollar Round Table with 9 Top of the Table and 19 Court of the Table honours and he has served in numerous volunteer positions within MDRT during his membership.

A financial consultant at Discovery, Logan is a UNISA BCOM graduate and a graduate of the Chartered Insurance Institute (London). He wrote and passed all four subjects at the inaugural exams of the Institute of Life and Pension Advisers (ILPA) in April 1982, becoming a Fellow of ILPA (FILPA) – it was subsequently converted to the CERTIFIED FINANCIAL PLANNER (CFP®) professional designation.

Logan is also a professional speaker and has presented nationally and internationally to tens of thousands of individuals, companies and organisations with a message based on encouragement, hope, self-mastery and vision. His main focus in the past, besides South Africa, has been India, where he has spoken extensively since 1996.

Logan speaking in Taipei at the 2015 MDRT DAY TAIWAN. He is also scheduled to do a virtual presentation at the 2022 MDRT DAY TAIWAN in April.

After intensive deliberation, and considering the essential nature of the Vedantic teachings, Logan enrolled for the three-year residential course at the Vedanta Academy in March 2016, graduating in 2019. He and Sussie left South Africa and relocated to Pune, India.

He has had an amazing experience studying and imbibing this profound knowledge with young seekers from all parts of the world. Logan wakes at 4:00 a.m. every day to study, exercises and does yoga seven days a week, has been a vegetarian since 2000 and on a vegan diet since 2013.

"Finish each day and be done with it. You have done what you could. Some blunders and absurdities no doubt crept in; forget them as soon as you can. Tomorrow is a new day. You shall begin it serenely and with too high a spirit to be encumbered with your old nonsense."

— Ralph Waldo Emerson

Logan's mission is to achieve inner transformation and to help empower individuals, families, communities and organisations to significantly enhance their human potential, productivity, peace of mind and quality of life.

He is married to Sussie and they have three daughters, Sarisha, Linestha and Nevita and three sons-in-law, Riyaz Bharucha, Vinay Chavan and Kunal Tulsiani.

Logan Naidu: Author, Life Coach & Speaker

Website: www.logannaidu.com

Email: logan@logannaidu.com

Some of those who have attended Logan's presentations had this to say:

"Logan is dynamic and inspirational. His presentations leave audiences on the edge of their seats... indeed, standing and applauding. He has a unique ability to synthesise the latest findings into a dynamic presentation suitable for all audiences: useful information conveyed in an entertaining format."

— **Peter Salovey, Ph.D.,** Chris Argyris Professor and Chair of Psychology, Yale University (Current President of Yale University)

"Logan is an inspiring and engaging presenter. He invites the audience to celebrate learning, laughter and personal leadership - live! I look forward to a chance to work with him again!"

> — **Joshua Freedman,** Director of Programmes, Six Seconds International eQ Network; editor, eQ TODAY: California, USA

"A powerful, energetic speaker who filled the room with such power and enthusiasm that you could feel the positive energy rushing up and down your body."

> — **Peter Rankin,** department store manager, South Africa

"I was so excited by your talk on visualization. Thank you very much for showing me the light. Your presence and presentations have been a source of great inspiration for me."

> — **Asis Bandyopadhyay,** AGM and principal, Corporate Training College, NICL, Kolkata, India

"Your motivational rendition at the World Consumer Rights Day kept all of us alive during the presentation."

> — **Mr Michael Mabuyakhulu,** minister: economic development and tourism, KwaZulu-Natal, South Africa

"The talk made me view life from a different angle and I hope whatever was said will stay in my heart for future use. The speaker reflected what he was saying, all the energy, the positiveness and attitude."

> — **Miss Lungile Hobe,** final year student, Nelson R Mandela School of Medicine, Durban, South Africa

"Logan is the most passionate, energetic and enthusiastic speaker that I have heard for many years. His presentation added enormous benefit to our delegates at Multirand Forum."

— **Mark Andries,** former chairman: Multirand Forum, South Africa

"Captivated the audience from right at the beginning of the talk. Your enthusiasm was infectious and I felt my attitude change to a more positive one as you progressed through the talk. Learnt some very important lessons, which I hope to take with me throughout my life. Very enjoyable; I was hoping the talk could go on. I am very inspired."

— **Miss Zanele Nkosi,** final year student, Nelson R Mandela School of Medicine, Durban, South Africa

"Perhaps the most dynamic speaker ever to grace an Estcourt platform; had the whole town buzzing after his motivational talk…"

— **Estcourt and Midlands News, South Africa**

"Logan's inspirational style and passion make his presentations a 'must see'."

— **Anthony Morris,** a leading training specialist

"I qualified for MDRT for the first time mainly and only because of Mr. Logan Naidu … he is an amazing personality."

— **Mannoj Rijhwaani,** Mumbai, India

"In 2002, Logan conducted a seminar on 'Double Your Productivity' in Mumbai. I attended that seminar, and it changed my life. From almost quitting the industry, I used Logan's principles to turbo charge my team, and 12 years on, I am ROCKING the business. Logan's enthusiasm for the business crept into my system. Going to the MDRT Annual Meeting this year! Thanks Logan, you did change my life."

— **Kapil Mathur,** Dubai, UAE